Vagus Nerve and Polyvagal Theory

---

2 Books in 1.

An Outstanding Guide and Exercises to Manage Emotional Stress, Overcome Anxiety and Depression, Heal Diseases and Inflammations

© Copyright 2020 by LAYNE KELLY
All rights reserved

This document is geared towards providing exact and reliable information with regard to the topic and issue covered. The publication is sold with the idea that the publisher is not required to render accounting, officially permitted or otherwise qualified services. If advice is necessary, legal, or professional, a practiced individual in the profession should be ordered. From a Declaration of Principles which was accepted and approved equally by a Committee of the American Bar Association and a Committee of Publishers and Associations.

In no way is it legal to reproduce, duplicate, or transmit any part of this document in either electronic means or in printed format. Recording of this publication is strictly prohibited and any storage of this document is not allowed unless with written permission from the publisher. All rights reserved.

The information provided herein is stated to be truthful and consistent, in that any liability, in terms of inattention or otherwise, by any usage or abuse of any policies, processes, or directions contained within is the solitary and utter responsibility of the recipient reader. Under no circumstances will any legal responsibility or blame be held against the publisher for any reparation, damages, or monetary loss due to the information herein, either directly or indirectly.

Respective authors own all copyrights not held by the publisher.

The information herein is offered for informational purposes solely and is universal as so. The presentation of the information is without a contract or any type of guarantee assurance.

The trademarks that are used are without any consent, and the publication of the trademark is without permission or backing by the trademark owner. All trademarks and brands within this book are for clarifying purposes only and are owned by the owners themselves, not affiliated with this document

TABLE OF CONTENTS

VAGUS NERVE (BOOK 1) 7

INTRODUCTION .... - 1 -

CHAPTER 1: THE VAGUS NERVE .... - 11 -

What happens when the vagus nerve isn't working admirably? .... - 13 -

Unlock the Powers of the Vagus Nerve .... - 16 -

CHAPTER 2: FUNCTION OF VAGUS NERVE AND POLYVAGAL THEORY .... - 20 -

Vagus Nerve Function .... - 21 -

Vagus Nerve Stimulation: How to Stimulate the Vagus Nerve Naturally .... - 24 -

Polyvagal Hypothesis .... - 29 -

Polyvagal Theory .... - 32 -

CHAPTER 3: DISEASES AND DISORDERS ASSOCIATED WITH VAGUS NERVE .... - 36 -

What Causes Vagus Nerve Disorders? .... - 38 -

Medications for Vagus Nerve Disorders .... - 40 -

CHAPTER 4: VAGUS NERVE AND SOCIAL ENGAGEMENT . - 45 -

The Social Engagement System .... - 45 -

Craniosacral Therapy .... - 48 -

CHAPTER 5: TAPPING INTO THE POWER OF THE VAGUS NERVE .... - 51 -

The Autonomic Nervous System (ANS) .... - 51 -

The Vagal Brake and Social Behavior .... - 55 -

CHAPTER 6: EXERCISE AND STIMULATION .... - 58 -

Vagus Nerve Stimulation Exercises .... - 58 -

Meditation - Mindfulness .... - 61 -

Yoga and Tai Chi .... - 62 -

CHAPTER 7: DIET AND VAGUS NERVE .... - 65 -

Nourishments for Making Acetylcholine .... - 65 -

Healthy Daily Routines for Vagus Nerve .... - 67 -

CONCLUSION .... - 73 -

THE POLYVAGAL THEORY (BOOK 2) .... - 74 -

INTRODUCTION .... - 76 -

CHAPTER ONE: POLYVAGAL THEORY IN PRACTICE .... - 78 -

Our three-section sensory system .... - 78 -

Injury's impact on sensory system reaction .... - 80 -

Explicit parts of ventral vagal nerve working .... - 81 -

Polyvagal theory .... - 82 -

CHAPTER TWO: POLYVAGAL THEORY AND HOW IT RELATES TO SOCIAL CUES .... - 85 -

The Body's Surveillance System .... - 85 -

Perusing Danger Cues .... - 86 -

The Vagus Nerve .... - 87 -

Three Developmental Stages of Response .... - 89 -

CHAPTER THREE: POLYVAGAL THEORY SIMPLIFIED ...... - 92 -

Association Mode .... - 94 -

Freeze, Flight, Fight, or Puff Up .... - 94 -

How injury influences the sensory system .... - 97 -

CHAPTER FOUR: CHILDREN, EMOTIONAL REGULATION, AND POLYVAGAL THEORY ....- 104 -

Being a sentiments analyst ....- 104 -

Polyvagal theory and kids ....- 105 -

Tools for passionate guideline ....- 107 -

Bringing up Resilient Children ....- 109 -

Strength is for Parents Too ....- 110 -

CHAPTER FIVE: POLYVAGAL THEORY AND ANXIETY ....- 112 -

Why Your Personal Narrative Adds To The Problem ....- 114 -

An Every Day Breathing Technique You Can Use Anywhere ....- 116 -

CHAPTER SIX: POLYVAGAL THEORY AND PTSD ....- 118 -

The Sensory System: A Basic Model ....- 118 -

Bioconductal Defenses ....- 119 -

The Vagal Brake ....- 120 -

The Social Sensory System ....- 120 -

Suggestions for Healing PTSD ....- 122 -

Settling Complex PTSD and Dissociation ....- 125 -

CHAPTER SEVEN: THE VAGAL PARADOX ....- 127 -

Consistency with Jacksonian Dissolution ....- 130 -

Different supporters of neuroception ....- 134 -

CHAPTER EIGHT: DORSAL VAGAL, FREEZE, AND POLYVAGAL SOLUTIONS .... - 135 -

The Role of the Dorsal Vagal and Pain .... - 136 -

Methodologies to Shift out of Maladaptive Defense States .... - 137 -

The Importance of Breathing and Movement .... - 140 -

The HPA (Hypothalamic Pituitary Adrenal Axis) .... - 143 -

Dread and Depression, Polyvagal Science, and Pain .... - 146 -

The Dorsal Vagal Shutdown .... - 153 -

CHAPTER NINE: CLINICAL APPLICATIONS OF THE POLYVAGAL THEORY .... - 158 -

Reframe Your Thinking Around Autism .... - 159 -

CHAPTER TEN: YOGA TREATMENT AND THE POLYVAGAL THEORY .... - 161 -

Vagal Activity, Interoception, Regulation, and Resilience .... - 166 -

Polyvagal Theory & Mind-Body Therapies for Regulation & Resilience .... - 168 -

SUMMARY .... - 170 -

CONCLUSION .... - 174 -

VAGUS NERVE

Easy Self-Help Exercises to Overcome Anxiety, Depression, Trauma, Chronic Diseases and Finally Improve Your Life

© Copyright 2019 by LAYNE KELLY
All rights reserved

This document is geared towards providing exact and reliable information with regard to the topic and issue covered. The publication is sold with the idea that the publisher is not required to render accounting, officially permitted or otherwise qualified services. If advice is necessary, legal, or professional, a practiced individual in the profession should be ordered. From a Declaration of Principles which was accepted and approved equally by a Committee of the American Bar Association and a Committee of Publishers and Associations.

In no way is it legal to reproduce, duplicate, or transmit any part of this document in either electronic means or in printed format. Recording of this publication is strictly prohibited and any storage of this document is not allowed unless with written permission from the publisher. All rights reserved.

The information provided herein is stated to be truthful and consistent, in that any liability, in terms of inattention or otherwise, by any usage or abuse of any policies, processes, or directions contained within is the solitary and utter responsibility of the recipient reader. Under no circumstances will any legal responsibility or blame be held against the publisher for any reparation, damages, or monetary loss due to the information herein, either directly or indirectly.

Respective authors own all copyrights not held by the publisher.

The information herein is offered for informational purposes solely and is universal as so. The presentation of the information is without a contract or any type of guarantee assurance.

The trademarks that are used are without any consent, and the publication of the trademark is without permission or backing by the trademark owner. All trademarks and brands within this book are for clarifying purposes only and are owned by the owners themselves, not affiliated with this document

INTRODUCTION

Vagus nerves also called X or tenth cranial nerve is the most prolonged and generally complex of the cranial nerves. The Vagus nerve originates from the brain through the face and thorax, to the ventral part of the abdomen. It's a blended nerve containing parasympathetic filaments. The vagus nerve has two tactile ganglia (masses of nerve tissue that transmit tangible driving forces): the predominant and the mediocre ganglia. The parts of the predominant ganglion innervate the skin in the concha of the ear. The substandard ganglion emits two branches: the pharyngeal nerve and the prevalent laryngeal nerve. The repetitive laryngeal nerve branches from the vagus in the lower neck and upper thorax to innervate the muscles of the larynx (voice box). The vagus additionally radiates cardiovascular, esophageal, and aspiratory branches. In the stomach area, the vagus innervates most of the stomach-related tract and other stomach viscera. The vagus nerve has the broadest dissemination of the cranial nerves. Its pharyngeal and laryngeal branches transmit engine driving forces to the pharynx and larynx; its cardiovascular branches act to slow the pace of heartbeat; its bronchial branch acts to contract the bronchi; and its esophageal branches control automatic muscles in the throat, stomach, gallbladder, pancreas, and small digestive system, animating peristalsis and gastrointestinal emissions. The Vagus nerve incitement, in which the nerve is invigorated with heartbeats of power, is sometimes utilized for patients with epilepsy or melancholy that is generally untreatable; the procedure has additionally been investigated for conditions such as Alzheimer malady and headache.

Cranial Nerves are a significant piece of the human body, as these nerves partake in a considerable most of the things we can do individually, for example, seeing, eating, and such like. These nerves emerge from the cerebrum or brainstem and exist two by two. They supply blood and sustenance to different organs in the head and the neck zones aside from the vagus nerve, which has an alternate capacity. There are 12 cranial nerves, and larger parts of them convey tangible strands. However, some cranial nerves convey engine filaments also and some convey both tactile and engine filaments.

Among the 12 cranial nerves, there are only 2 nerves that emerge from the cerebellum, while the rest emerge from the brainstem. These cranial nerves have been named dependent on their capacities and structure. Outlined underneath are the rundown of the cranial nerves and their capacities in detail.As expressed above, there are 12 cranial nerves. These cranial nerves are:

Olfactory Nerve

As the name proposes, this nerve manages the feeling of smell; the receptors of these nerves are situated in the nasal mucosa. This is the most limited nerve among the entirety of the cranial nerves and it doesn't enter the brainstem.

Optic Nerve

Again, as the name recommends, this nerve manages vision; meaning, what we can see and not see. This nerve emerges from the retina of the eye and sends visual signs to the cerebrum, which frames an image of the objects we see. This nerve is viewed as a piece of the fringe sensory system. Any harm or damage to this nerve can prompt a total loss of vision either briefly or forever relying upon the damage caused to the nerve.

Oculomotor Nerve

The Oculomotor Nerve comes third in the rundown of the 12 cranial nerves pursued by the olfactory and the optic nerve. The capacity of this cranial nerve is to control eyeball and eyelid development. This nerve has two-engine part, which have their own particular capacities and are physical engine segment and instinctive engine segment.

Trochlear Nerve

This is otherwise called Cranial Nerve IV and it's the fourth in the rundown of cranial nerves. This is the main cranial nerve that emerges dorsally from the cerebrum. This nerve additionally gives its support to the eye. The principle capacity of this nerve is to give it the capacity to roll the eyes here and there and furthermore outwards.

Trigeminal Nerve

The trigeminal nerve is one of most significant cranial nerves. It has three branches to be specific; these are the ophthalmic, maxillary, and mandibular. Each branch interfaces nerves from the mind to the various pieces of the face. The primary capacity of the trigeminal nerve is to give sensations to the mouth, teeth, face, and the nasal hole. This nerve likewise controls the nerve that enables us to bite in nourishment.

Abducens Nerve

This nerve is likewise called as Cranial Nerve VI. The principle capacity of this cranial nerve is to permit development of the eyes sideways significance away from the nose. Any damage to this nerve can bring about an individual having obscured or twofold vision.

Facial Nerve

The facial nerve is likewise called as Cranial Nerve VII. It has to be two elements in specific, of which one is to convey tactile sign from the tongue to the inside part of the mouth and furthermore this nerve helps an individual produce outward appearance.

Vestibulocochlear Nerve

As the name proposes, this cranial nerve has functions of incorporating two pieces, of which initially is the feeling of hearing, which is the cochlear part and the second is simply the capacity of a person to adjust himself or herself, which shapes the vestibular part. Any harm or damage to this cranial nerve may bring about loss of hearing or offset issues with the influenced person.

Glossopharyngeal Nerve

The Glossopharyngeal Nerve is the ninth cranial nerve that is available in the body. This nerve begins from the brainstem, navigates through the base of the skull, and ends at the mouth in the mucous organs and base of the tongue. This nerve has different branches; these are the tonsillar branch, tympanic branch, stylopharyngeal branch, carotid sinus nerve branch, and the lingual branch. Since it partitions into numerous branches, then it must have different capacities. It gets tactile filaments from the pieces of the tongue, carotids, tonsils, and the center ear. It likewise innervates the parasympathetic filaments that help in assimilation and resting of the body. It additionally innervates the engine strands of the stylopharyngeus muscle, which helps in gulping.

Vagus Nerve

This cranial nerve is the longest of every cranial nerve and starts from the brainstem, crosses right down to the mid-region passing the heart, lungs, and throat in transit. This cranial nerve shapes a piece of the automatic sensory system and controls the body strategies, which are not in the control of an individual like controlling the pulse and supporting in nourishment assimilation. Incitement of the vagus nerve is a favored treatment for patients with epilepsy and melancholy. Incitement of the vagus nerve because of eruption of the body to specific upgrades prompts a condition called vasovagal syncope or blacking out scenes, as this incitement causes a drop in circulatory strain and pulse.

Adornment Nerve

This is the eleventh cranial nerve of the 12 that exist in the human body. This nerve controls the development of the muscles of the neck. There are two pieces of the Accessory Nerve, which are the spinal and cranial divisions, of which the cranial subdivision is ignored. The spinal adornment nerve gives capacity to the sternocleidomastoid muscle, the upper back, and the shoulder. Any brokenness of this cranial nerve may prompt the shoulders and neck not performing to the ideal level.

Hypoglossal Nerve

The Hypoglossal Nerve is the remainder of the cranial nerves. The fundamental capacity of this cranial nerve is to control developments of the tongue. This nerve begins in the brainstem, navigates through the carotid supply route and jugular vein, and winds up underneath the tongue. Any harm or damage to the hypoglossal nerve may make the tongue totally incapacitated bringing about instance where the individual would not be able to eat or talk appropriately. There are numerous and various causes, which can harm the hypoglossal nerve, for example, a contamination or damage to the nerve bringing about the tongue being incapacitated.

Autonomic sensory system and enteric sensory system

The autonomic sensory system manages an assortment of body process that happens without cognizant exertion. The autonomic framework is the relevant part of the fringe sensory system that is answerable for controlling automatic body capacities, for example, heartbeat, blood stream, breathing, and assimilation.

The Structure of the Autonomic Nervous System

This framework is additionally separated into three branches, namely: the thoughtful framework, the parasympathetic framework, and the enteric sensory system.

- The thoughtful division of the autonomic sensory system directs the flight-or-battle reactions. This division likewise performs such assignments as loosening up the bladder, accelerating pulse, and expanding student's eye.
- The parasympathetic division of the autonomic sensory system helps keep up with the ordinary body capacities and rations physical assets. This division additionally performs such errands

as controlling the bladder, hindering pulse, and tightening eye understudies.

The autonomic sensory system is additionally comprised of a third part, known as the enteric sensory system, which is bound to the gastrointestinal tract. The autonomic sensory system works by accepting data from the earth and from different pieces of the body. The thoughtful and parasympathetic frameworks will in general have contradicting activities in which one framework will animate a reaction and where the other will hinder it. Generally, incitement has been thought to happen through the thoughtful framework while restraint was thought to happen by means of the parasympathetic framework. Anyway, numerous special cases to this have been found. For instance, the thoughtful sensory system will act to raise pulse, while the parasympathetic sensory system will act to bring down it. The two frameworks work in relation to deal with the body's reactions relying on the circumstance and need. In the event that, for instance, you are confronting a danger and need to escape, the thoughtful framework will rapidly assemble your body to make a move. When the danger has passed, the parasympathetic framework will at that point begin to hose these reactions, gradually restoring your body to its typical, resting state.

What Does the Autonomic Nervous System Do?

The autonomic framework controls an assortment of inward procedures including:

- Digestion
- Blood pressure
- Heart rate
- Urination and crap
- Pupillary reaction
- Breathing (respiratory) rate
- Sexual reaction
- Body temperature

- Metabolism
- Electrolyte balance
- Production of body liquids including sweat and salivation
- Emotional reactions

The autonomic nerve pathways associate with various organs to the cerebrum stem or spinal line. There are additionally two key synapses, or compound flag-bearers, that are significant for correspondence inside the autonomic sensory system:

- Acetylcholine is regularly utilized in the parasympathetic framework to have a repressing impact.
- Norepinephrine regularly works inside the thoughtful framework to affect stimulatingly the body.

How the Autonomic Nervous System Works

At the point when the parasympathetic and thoughtful parts of the autonomic sensory systems become out of match, individuals can encounter an autonomic issue, likewise called dysautonomia. There are various kinds of autonomic issue, each with its very own interesting arrangement of side effects, including:

- Acute autonomic loss of motion
- Afferent baroreflex disappointment
- Idiopathic orthostatic hypotension
- Multiple framework decay
- Orthostatic hypotension
- Postprandial hypotension
- Pure autonomic disappointment
- Familial dysautonomia (Riley-Day disorder)
- Secondary orthostatic hypotension

These scatters can happen alone, or because of different conditions, that causes disturbance in the autonomic sensory system, including:

- Autoimmune malady

- Alcohol or medication misuse
- Diabetes
- Parkinson's malady
- Cancer
- Chronic exhaustion disorder
- Peripheral neuropathy
- Aging
- Spinal line issue
- Trauma

Symptoms

If you or somebody you love is encountering disturbances in the autonomic sensory system, you may encounter at least one of the accompanying manifestations. A few people experience one bunch of manifestations one after another and another arrangement of side effects on different occasions. The manifestations can be short-lived and eccentric or activated by explicit circumstances or activities, as in the wake of ingesting certain nourishments or subsequent to standing up rapidly.

- Dizziness or tipsiness after standing
- Fatigue and idleness
- Erectile brokenness
- Lack of sweat or lavish perspiring
- Urinary incontinence
- Difficulty purging the bladder
- Lack of pupillary reaction
- Disturbing a throbbing painfulness
- Faintness (or even genuine blacking out spells)
- Tachycardia (quick pulse)
- Hypotension Gastrointestinal manifestations
- Numbness and shivering
- Severe tension or misery

Enteric sensory system

The enteric sensory system is really a second cerebrum that numerous individuals never realized they had. Even though it has not been experimentally demonstrated and contemplated up until recently as of late, we have all had the experience of having certain premonitions about a circumstance or of having butterflies in our stomach when we are anxious about something. Nevertheless, notwithstanding the fact that these sentiments alongside different stomach related manifestations, we've not paid attention to it as well; we are currently finding out that, the cells and tissues in our stomach really have "a brain of their own" and that we should start paying attention to its messages more. One of the intriguing things that were found when concentrating on the enteric framework was that, similar synapses that are available in the cerebrum moved to the gut also. By discovering that synthetic concoctions, for example, serotonin, dopamine, glutamate, and norepinephrine are situated inside our enteric sensory system, doctors and researchers have had no real option except to recognize the way that there is some genuine premise to our premonitions and responses that have, up until this point, been genuinely difficult to clarify. These discoveries have approved these "hunches," yet they additionally assume a significant job in helping us explore our very own lives just as in treating different issues of the stomach related tract. Although our enteric framework makes up a subsequent cerebrum, this doesn't imply that the two structures are working as isolated substances. Actually, the two cerebrums are connected intensely and influence each other in numerous respects. This implies that feeling anxious or being placed in an unpleasant or awkward circumstance will unavoidably cause some piece of intestinal pain and that issues in our stomach can cause a lot of mental uneasiness too. In view of the potential ramifications of the enteric sensory system and what we ordinarily consider as our cerebrum, these two zones of the body should be contemplated independently just as related to each other. Despite the fact that there is still a lot to find out about our enteric sensory system, we can at present utilize the ebb and flow, looking into in reducing intestinal and mental trouble, just as helping us to run our lives even more beneficially. By realizing that our hunches are similarly as substantial as any thoughts that we think of intelligently, we can really tune in to the data given to us by our enteric framework. On the other side, we can use our brain to help mend issues happening in our stomach related tract.

CHAPTER 1: The Vagus Nerve

As said, the vagus nerve is one of the two cranial nerves that are incredibly long, reaching out from the mind stem, right to the viscera. The vagus nerves convey a wide arrangement of sign to and from the mind, and they are liable for various natural reactions in the body. You may likewise hear the vagus nerve called Cranial Nerve X, as it is the tenth cranial nerve or the Wandering Nerve. A lot of research has been done on the vagus nerve, as it is an entrancing cranial nerve.

Vagus is Latin for "meandering," and it is an exact portrayal of this nerve, which rises at the back of the skull and wanders in a comfortable manner through the mid-region, with various stretching nerves encountering the heart, lungs, voicebox, stomach, and ears, among other body parts. The vagus nerve conveys approaching data from the sensory system to the mind, giving data about what the body is doing, and it likewise transmits active data, which administers a scope of reflex reactions.

The vagus nerve directs the heartbeat, control muscle development, keeps the individual breathing, and transmit an assortment of synthetics through the body. It is likewise liable for keeping the stomach-related tract in working request, getting the muscles of the stomach and digestion tracts to help process nourishment, and sending back data about what is being processed and what the body is receiving in return.

At the point when the vagus nerve is invigorated, the reaction is frequently a decrease in pulse or relaxing. Now and again, unreasonable incitement can make somebody have what is known as a vaso-vagal reaction, seeming to fall into a blackout or extreme lethargies since their pulse and circulatory strain drop to such an extent. Particular incitement of this nerve is likewise utilized in some medicinal treatment; vagus incitement seems to profit individuals who experience the ill effects of sorrow, for instance, it is additionally once in a while used to treat epilepsy.

You typically don't see the activities of the privilege and left vagus nerves, yet you presumably would see if this nerve stopped working because of infection or injury, in light of the fact that the vagus nerve is one of the numerous crucial nerves which keeps your body in working request. Without the elements of the vagus nerve, you would see that it's hard to talk, inhale, or eat, and your pulse would turn out to be incredibly unpredictable.

We can separate the elements of the vagus nerve into four key zones:

Parasympathetic

This is liable for substantial capacities while we are very still. Consider things like assimilation, metabolic procedures, and pulse. It has likewise been portrayed as the "bolster and breed" or "rest and overview" framework for its job in salivation, sexual excitement, processing, and pee.

Sensory

This process tangible data from the heart, lungs, stomach area, and throat

Motor

The vagus nerve gives development to the neck muscles that are liable for discourse and gulping.

Special tangible

It gives taste sensation behind the tongue.

There are numerous imperative capacities that are affected by the vagus nerve, for instance; keeping a consistent pulse, breathing, perspiring, managing circulatory strain and blood glucose, advancing kidney capacity, and ripeness. It sends data about the condition of your internal organs to your cerebrum. Essentially, it is assisting with significant capacities that keep us alive.

What happens when the vagus nerve isn't working admirably?

A little examination into the vagus nerve finds an entire host of conditions that have either been emphatically connected or are as of now being explored for a connect to the nerve. These range from minor inconveniences to significant issues. Obviously, on the off chance that you are affected anywhere on a range, it can influence your general sentiment of prosperity and general execution.

The vast majority will encounter a vasovagal reaction because of a stressor or overstimulation of the vagus nerve sooner or later. Circulatory strain brings down pulse, eases back, and the veins in your legs broaden, which can cause sickness or blacking out. This is a, for the most part, an innocuous reaction which leaves without anyone else, be that as it may, a few people who experience it all the more incessantly may need to look for restorative assistance.

Some different issues connected with vagus nerve brokenness include stoutness, tension, temperament issue, bradycardia, gastrointestinal infections, incessant irritation, swooning, and seizures.

Obviously, the greater part of these conditions illustrated can prompt further ailment, for instance, corpulence and aggravation are both connected with diseases and diabetes. Tension or mindset issue may likewise prompt despondency.

How does "hacking" the vagus work?

There is a developing assortment of research to recommend that we can control or "hack" the vagus nerve. Vagus hacks go back to some research directed in the year 1998. Through this work, it was found that by invigorating the vagus nerve with an electrical drive could decrease the body's incendiary reaction.

This has positive ramifications for the treatment conditions, for example, Crohn's Disease, rheumatoid joint inflammation, and other incendiary infections. Tracey's exploration frames the premise of the thought for bioelectronics, which we currently observe when treating the condition. for example, discouragement and epilepsy.

Outside of those conditions, aggravation is a reaction that we as a whole have in our bodies, regularly because of stress. For certain individuals, pressure and fiery reaction can get incessant, prompting other medical problems.

The vagus nerve is connected to such a significant number of various capacities, that there are more "hacks" than having a bioelectric gadget embedded to animate it (this is typically just for extraordinary cases). Truth be told, specialists have discovered that we can battle aggravation by connecting with the vagus nerve and improving "vagal tone," like an exercise!

How about we take a gander at what you can be doing:

Work on your passionate wellbeing

A recent report found that a high vagal tone was a piece of a criticism circle between physical wellbeing, positive feelings, and positive social associations. These elements influence each other with a self-supporting dynamic.

During the examination, members utilized Loving Kindness Meditation (LKM) as an approach to affect emphatically their passionate wellbeing. The analysts likewise found out that when individuals thought about positive social associations or attempted to improve their bonds with different people, it beneficially affected vagal tone.

Work on gut wellbeing

Did you realize that "hunch" is a genuine article? A sign from the vagus nerve go from the gut to the cerebrum. This has been connected to regulating state of mind and a few sorts of dread and uneasiness. An indication of a solid vagal tone is somebody who has elegance, under strain characteristic that most business visionaries could utilize!

Your vagus nerve is continually sending refreshed tangible data about the condition of your body's organs, stomach-related tract, pulse, and other data, up to your mind by means of various nerves. There is research to show that our gut organisms and those pathways to the cerebrum are interlinked. It is likewise imagined that gut microbiota are the potential key modulator of the invulnerable and the sensory systems. In this manner, keeping up a solid gut is a vagus "hack."

The takeaway: Gut wellbeing differs from individual to individual and relies upon how you are manufactured, yet by and large, you can take probiotics, eat sound, have adjusted eating routine of entire nourishments, evade pointless utilization of anti-infection agents, and moderate utilization of sugary food sources or liquor. As a further note, while probiotics are yet being investigated for their potential, a Canadian report saw them as a viable PTSD treatment. There are additional suggestions for the treatment of stress - investigating whether you can profit by taking them might be a straightforward advance you can take.

The vagus nerve assumes a fundamental job in our general wellbeing and prosperity. As a businessperson, you've presumably felt the impacts of the physiological reactions it oversees without acknowledging it – especially during distressing periods.

"Hacking" your vagus nerve is extremely about embracing a couple of solid practices that keep it invigorated and working ideally. There are more procedures we could plunge into, yet those recorded are the absolute least, difficult to execute and have strong logical sponsorship. You can take full breaths from your office!

In the event that you do happen to experience the ill effects of one of the more constant incendiary conditions, vagus nerve incitement through electrical driving forces shows a great deal of guarantee. This might be something to examine and rise with your medicinal expert.

Unlock the Powers of the Vagus Nerve

The vagus nerve shouldn't be stunned into shape. It can likewise be conditioned and fortified like a muscle. Here are some outstanding practices you can do that may improve your wellbeing notably:

Positive Social Relationships

An examination had members contemplate, others while quietly, rehashed positive expressions about loved ones, contrasted with the controls. The meditators demonstrated a general increment in positive feelings like peacefulness, satisfaction, and expectation subsequent to finishing the class. These positive musings of others prompted an improvement in the vagal capacity as found in pulse inconstancy. The outcomes likewise demonstrated a more conditioned vagus nerve than when pondering.

Cold

Cold presentation, for example, cool showers, or face dunking animates the nerve also.

Studies show that when your body changes with chilly, your battle or flight (thoughtful) framework decays, your rest, condensation (parasympathetic) framework increments, and this are intervened by the vagus nerve. Any sort of intense cold presentation including drinking super cold water will build vagus nerve initiation.

Swishing

Another home solution for an under-invigorated vagus nerve is to rinse the body with water. Washing really invigorates the muscles of the bed, which are terminated by the vagus nerve.

"Ordinarily, patients will destroy a piece, which is a decent sign and on the off chance that they don't, we prescribe that they do it normally, then consistently until they see that they do fire destroying a piece," says Hoffman. "This has been appeared to promptly improve working memory execution."

Singing and Chanting

Humming, mantra reciting, song singing, and peppy vivacious singing, all expand pulse fluctuation (HRV) in somewhat various ways. Basically, singing resembles starting a vagal siphon conveying loosening up waves. Singing as loud as possible works the muscles in the back of the throat to actuate the vagus. Singing as one, this is regularly done in houses of worship and synagogues, additionally builds HRV and vagus work. Singing has been found to build oxytocin, otherwise called the adoration hormone, since it makes individuals feel more like each other.

Backrub

You can invigorate your vagus nerve by rubbing your feet and your neck along the carotid sinus, situated along the carotid veins on either side of your neck. A neck and back rub can help diminish seizures. A foot rub can bring down your pulse and circulatory strain. A weight back rub can likewise enact the vagus nerve. These back rubs are utilized to assist newborn children with putting on weight by invigorating gut work, to a great extent, intervened by initiating the vagus nerve.

Chuckling

Happiness and giggling are common resistant promoters. Giggling likewise invigorates the vagus nerve. Research shows how chuckling expands HRV in a gathering domain.

There are different case reports of individuals blacking out from giggling, and this might be from the vagus nerve/parasympathetic framework being animated excessively. Blacking out can come after giggling just as pee, hacking, gulping, or solid discharge - which are all aided along by vagus enactment.

Yoga & Tai Chi

Both have increment on vagus nerve action and your parasympathetic framework when all is said and done. Studies have demonstrated that yoga builds GABA, a quieting synapse in your mind. Scientists trust it does this by "invigorating vagal afferents (filaments)," which increment movement in the parasympathetic sensory system. This is particularly useful for individuals who battle with uneasiness or misery. Studies show that jujitsu additionally can 'upgrade vagal adjustment.'

Breathing Deeply & Slowly

Your heart and neck contain neurons that have receptors called baroreceptors, which identify the circulatory strain and transmit the neuronal sign to your cerebrum. This enacts your vagus nerve that associates with your heart to bring down circulatory strain and pulse. Slow breathing, with a generic equivalent measure of time taking in and out, expands the affectability of baroreceptors and vagal enactment. Breathing around 5-6 breaths for every moment in the normal grown-up can be exceptionally useful.

Exercise

Exercise expands your cerebrum's development hormone, bolsters your mind's mitochondria, and helps switch psychological decay. On the other hand, it's been appeared to animate the vagus nerve, which prompts valuable cerebrum and psychological well-being impacts. Gentle exercise additionally invigorates the gut stream, which is interceded by the vagus nerve.

Espresso Enemas

Enemas resembles run for your vagus nerve. Growing the gut builds vagus nerve enactment, as it finished with douches. This purging is cultivated by expanding the liver's ability to detoxify poisons in the blood and restricting them to the bile. All the while, the liver purges itself as it discharges the dangerous bile into the little, at that point huge, digestive tract for clearing. The whole blood supply courses through the liver at regular intervals. By holding the espresso 12 to 15 minutes, the blood will circle four to multiple times for purifying, much like a dialysis treatment. The water substance of the espresso invigorates the intestinal peristalsis and discharges the internal organ with the aggregated poisonous bile.

Electrical Wave Stimulation

There are wearable items that send a delicate electrical wave through the left ear channel to animate the body's vagus nerve while synchronizing with music, which thusly invigorates the arrival of synapses in the cerebrum that create a quieting sensation all through the body.

Unwind

Learning how to chill might be the No. 1 thing to help keep your vagus nerve conditioned. As indicated by Hoffman, most loosening up exercises will animate the vagus nerve.

CHAPTER 2: Function of Vagus Nerve and Polyvagal Theory

People have an Autonomic Nervous System (ANS) that is really included three separate subsystems, the Parasympathetic Nervous System (PNS), the Sympathetic Nervous System (SNS) and the Enteric Nervous System (ENS). The enteric sensory system has been depicted as a "second mind," which speaks with the focal sensory system (CNS) through the parasympathetic (e.g., by means of the vagus nerve) and thoughtful sensory systems. In any case, vertebrate examinations show that when the vagus nerve is cut off, the enteric sensory system keeps on working.

We presently realize that the ENS isn't only equipped for self-sufficiency yet additionally influences the cerebrum. Indeed, around 90 percent of the signs going along the vagus nerve come not from above, yet from the ENS, and that is the reason many consider it as a reinforcement mind focused on our sun-powered plexus. Our gut senses are not dreams but genuine apprehensive signs that guides quite a bit of our lives. Our vagus nerve gives the entryway between the two pieces of the autonomic frameworks. The vagus goes about as a bio-educational information transport that courses our motivations going in two ways. Since the vagus nerve goes about as the focal switchboard, it should not shock anyone that debilitated working of this one nerve can prompt such huge numbers of various conditions and issues. Some neurological infections really come up from the gut, spreading to the cerebrum by means of the vagus nerve. The vagus nerve is the president with regards to having beauty under strain. The autonomic sensory system contains two perfect inverse frameworks that make a reciprocal back-and-forth. This enables your body to look after homeostasis (inward soundness). The thoughtful sensory system is outfitted to fire you up like the gas pedal in a car – it blossoms with adrenaline and cortisol and it's a piece of the battle or flight reaction. The parasympathetic sensory system is the total inverse. The vagus nerve is directional fundamentally for the capacity of the parasympathetic sensory system. Lamentably, the vagus nerve's reflexive reactions can reverse discharge and divert it from companion into saboteur.

Vagus Nerve Function

The vagus nerve has a broad capacity in the body and it is situated all through the chest area. The long cranial nerve is that vagus nerve that associates the mind to the gut.

The vagus nerve additionally helps the heart and your interior organs to work appropriately. Poorly vagal nerve connects frequently with stomach related issues, poor rest wellbeing, exhaustion, and nervousness.

We would glance in more in details at how the vagus nerve capacities and how vagal tone can influence your wellbeing.

Vagus nerve work in the mind

Your vagal nerve assumes a significant job in how your brain functions.

Specialists have discovered that the vagus nerve is the principal association between the cerebrum and gastrointestinal tract and sends data about the condition of the internal organs to the mind. Studies show that vagus nerve work is likewise associated with mental conditions.

Specialists from the Mayo Clinic states that overseeing epilepsy is one reason why there are gadgets to animate the vagal nerve. The animating impact on the vagus nerve sends a sign to the cerebrum and can diminish the recurrence of seizures.

Vagus nerve work and your mind-set

Since your vagal tone is firmly associated with your mind work, it isn't astounding that your vagus nerve influences your mind-set.

Neuroscientists agreed in 2018 upon the poor capacity of the vagus nerve, that it could prompt the mind-set and tension issues. At times, it is conceivable to animate the vagus nerve by improving your gut wellbeing. The expansion in vagal tone can likewise help direct pressure and lighten restless emotions.

Vagus nerve influences your gut wellbeing

Stress and nervousness frequently cause stomach-related miracle because of the manner in which the vagus nerve interfaces the cerebrum and gut.

Specialists call the capacity of the vagus nerve the "gut-cerebrum hub." Stress represses the vagus nerve capacity and influences your stomach-related wellbeing. This vagal brokenness can prompt different stomach related issues brought about by aggravation and poor gut microbiota.

Sometimes, animating the vagus nerve in the gut utilizing probiotics could be a novel method to improve vagal tone. This can treat manifestations of vagus nerve brokenness, for example, bad-tempered inside disorder (IBS) and fiery gut illness (IBD). Then again, invigorating the vagus nerve work in the mind through unwinding procedures, profound breathing, or intercession can positively affect your gut's wellbeing.Different examinations have demonstrated that vagus incitement ensures there is sufficient stomach corrosive for processing. Vagus nerve work additionally influences levels of an inborn factor (a kind of protein known as though) in your gut, which is expected to counteract a nutrient B12 lack.

Vagus nerve capacity and craving

The impact of vagus nerve work on your stomach-related framework can likewise control your hunger. The diary Gastroenterology reports that vagus movement assumes a job in managing your craving. Analysts have discovered that one of the vagus nerve harm manifestations is weight.Different examinations point to the way that an appropriately working vagus nerve additionally builds sentiments of satiety. Your vagal tone transports sign to your cerebrum, making you feel fuller and may help keep you from gorging. Be that as it may, scientists clarify that the vagus nerve work is incredibly mind-boggling and confused, and there is little proof to propose that vagus nerve incitement treats corpulence or lower body weight.

Vagus nerve work and your interior organs

Your left and right vagus nerves are associated with the greater part of your inward organs and assist them with working appropriately. For instance, some researchers gave an account of an investigation demonstrating that an expansion in vagus movement can help decrease cardiovascular breakdown. Specialists found that utilizing a gadget to animate the vagus nerve expanded nitric oxygen levels and brought down aggravation. Both of these are significant in boosting heart wellbeing.Research likewise shows that vagal nerve action influences bladder work.

Solid vagal nerve work is likewise important for the kidneys to work appropriately and channel poisons likewise. Examinations have demonstrated that invigorating the vagus nerve improves blood course through the kidneys.

Vagus nerve work influences aggravation

A significant motivation to ensure that you have great vagal tone is to lessen irritation in your body. Albeit, momentary irritation is important to treat diseases and help the body recuperate itself. Long haul aggravation can be hindering to your wellbeing. Incessant aggravation has been connected to illnesses, for example, coronary illness, sensitivities, diabetes, and malignant growth.Concentrates into the manner in which the vagus nerve capacities have demonstrated, that is, it helps lower provocative reactions. Researchers conjectured that improving the vagus nerve capacity could help oversee aggravation related ailments. Preliminaries have demonstrated that expanded vagus nerve action could help oversee confusions related to corpulence, diabetes, immune system conditions, and poor cardiovascular wellbeing.

Vagus Nerve Stimulation: How to Stimulate the Vagus Nerve Naturally

What is vagus nerve incitement and by what means can improve vagal tone help direct many-body capacities? Researchers state that incitement of the vagal nerve can allude to any procedure to increment vagal action. There are different strategies for invigorating the vagus nerve to help support your wellbeing. For instance, breathing activities, vigorous working out, back rub, and yoga have all appeared to help and improve vagal tone. A portion of the advantages of invigorating your vagus nerve incorporate bringing down circulatory strain, improving cardiovascular wellbeing, getting a charge out of better rest, diminishing tension, and boosting mental wellbeing.

We should glance in more detail at the logical proof on the different ways you can animate the vagus nerve. Sprinkling cold water all over or putting a virus sodden washcloth on the back of your neck can cause vagus nerve incitement. Studies have indicated that being presented to cold temperatures builds vagus action. An intense introduction to the virus discharges certain synapses in the gastrointestinal framework that influence mental wellbeing. Different examinations have indicated that an expansion in vagus nerve movement brought about by acclimatization to the virus, which helps parasympathetic action. This is the place pulse backs off and muscles in the gastrointestinal tract unwind, once in a while alluded to as the "rest-and-summary" impact.

Murmur or Sing to Stimulate the Vagus Nerve

Singing in the shower, singing in an ensemble, or simply murmuring along to your main tune can advance great wellbeing through vagus nerve incitement.

In a study including adults, vocalists found out that singing in a gathering influences pulse fluctuation. Scientists found that singing requires guided breathing which can influence vagal tone. This sort of breathing improves the vagal reaction and improves prosperity.

Cognizant Breathing Benefits Vagus Nerve Function

Profound breathing activities where you deliberately control air admission and yield can help unwind and animate the vagal reaction. The diary Frontiers in Psychology detailed that cognizant breathing cause's vagus nerve incitement. Breathing in profoundly, and afterward breathing out gradually hinders the pulse and lower circulatory strain.

One investigation found out that doing breathing-activities for 15 minutes per day for about fourteen days significantly affected the measure of air individuals with incessant cardiovascular breakdown could breathe out. Different investigations show that breathing activities decidedly influence the vagal tone and can improve enthusiastic and mental wellbeing.

Yoga Stimulation for the Vagus Nerve

Numerous yoga practices include cognizant, conscious breathing and can improve vagal tone. An examination including sound grown-ups found out that moderate breathing and getting the throat muscles help to improve vagal reactions. The yoga procedures bring down circulatory strain and reduce tension. Another way that yoga practices help to animate the vagus nerve is by utilizing "OM" reciting, the vibration that the reciting or murmuring makes, build vagus action and unwinds. To discover more, just keep reading, as I will explain several other numerous medical issues you can fix by utilizing some straightforward yoga presents, just as this yoga for complete amateurs.

Mellow Exercising for Vagus Nerve Stimulation

Customary physical activity is useful for your cardiovascular wellbeing and helps in supporting vagal activity. One of the advantages that practicing has on vagus nerve incitement is to your stomach-related wellbeing. Analysts have found that mellow practicing advances sound vagal tone. This invigorates the gastric muscles and prompting better assimilation. Specialists have discovered that invigorating the "gut-mind hub" enables the stomach to process nourishment better. You can find out about other regular approaches to improve your stomach related wellbeing in the event that you have a blockage or other assimilation issues.

Probiotics Can Affect the Vagus Nerve and Improve Gut Function

You can resolve a large number of indications of vagal brokenness by taking probiotics to improve your gut microbiota. There are numerous examinations demonstrating that probiotics can support your stomach-related wellbeing. Some portion of the motivation behind why probiotics are useful for your processing is that they invigorate your vagus nerve.

One examination found out that taking Lactobacillus rhamnosus probiotic could improve your gastrointestinal wellbeing. Since your gut's wellbeing likewise influences your state of mind and cerebrum works through the vagus nerve, probiotics can likewise oversee pressure, tension, and sadness.I will explain some answers concerning the numerous motivations to take probiotics consistently, which sort of probiotics reestablishes gut verdure in the wake of taking anti-infection agents.

Omega-3 Affects Heart Function and the Vagus Nerve

Taking fish oil enhancements can increment vagal movement and positively affect your cardiovascular wellbeing. There are many studies indicating how omega-3 cases can keep your heart sound, lessen irritation, and emphatically influence your state of mind. Will taking omega-3 enhancements animate your vagus nerve? One investigation including men, found that taking omega-3 unsaturated fats animated the vagal nerve. Over a 4-month time span, the men had a lower pulse and better recuperation after exercise when normally taking omega-3 enhancements.

Different investigations have indicated that taking omega-3 normally likewise builds pulse changeability and lessens the danger of cardiovascular sickness.

Back rub to stimulate the Vagus Nerve

One of the advantages of having a back rub to assist you with unwinding is that its increments vagal action in your body. Gadgets intended to animate the vagus nerve are at times used to control epilepsy seizures. Notwithstanding, rubbing the carotid sinus on the sides of your neck can have a comparable impact.

Clinical studies revealed that kneading the carotid sinus could smother seizures as it animates the vagus nerve. Different specialists state that a carotid sinus rubs increments vagal tone. Physicians reported that a certified therapeutic expert typically completes a carotid sinus rub. Invigorating the vagus nerve in such a manner can decrease a fast heartbeat and lower circulatory strain rapidly. There are best basic oils to use in a loosening up back rub to help cut your feelings of anxiety down?

Foot Reflexology to Regulate Vagus Nerve Function

Rubbing your feet benefits your general prosperity since it is another approach to animate your vagus nerve. One little examination found out that foot reflexology increments vagal tone and has numerous advantages for your cardiovascular framework. Rubbing explicit zones of the foot brings down circulatory strain normally and gives advantages to individuals with coronary illness.

Discontinuous Fasting to Improve Vagus Nerve Function

This is one approach to invigorate your vagus nerve normally and advantage your pulse changeability is to fasten it irregularly. Discontinuous fasting is now and then called the 5:2 eating regimen. This includes eating regularly for 5 days and afterward on 2 non eating days back to back days, having a fractional quick. Calorie consumption for the fasting days ought to be 500 calories for women and 600 calories for men. Studies have demonstrated that irregular fasting is a compelling method to get more fit and keep up with weight reduction. The impacts of fasting on the vagus nerve influence the yearning hormone ghrelin.

Different investigations have indicated that fasting is an approach to animate the capacity of the vagus nerve. On the off chance that you need to get in shape rapidly, find out about the advantages of discontinuous fasting to help shed pounds of muscle versus fat.

Different Methods to Stimulate the Vagus Nerve and Affect its Function

There are different approaches to improve vagal tone for better wellbeing and prosperity:

Chuckling animates the vagus nerve

There is some logical support to the platitude that giggling is the best prescription. The diary Alternative Therapies in Health and Medicine distributed an examination on the impacts of yoga snickering on pulse fluctuation. Controlled giggling sessions diminished uneasiness and lift the mind-set.

Serotonin supplements influence vagus nerve work

Taking enhancements, for example, 5-HTP can support serotonin levels in the cerebrum and increment vagal action. Studies have indicated that 5-HTP supplements help to invigorate the vagus nerve. This can likewise help with bringing down sadness, lessening hypertension, and boosting your state of mind.

Discover what other common fixings help to support levels of serotonin.

Needle therapy to manage the vagus nerve

One reason why needle therapy is useful for your general wellbeing and prosperity is that it invigorates the vagal nerve. Studies have demonstrated that needle therapy manages vagal action and improves your gastrointestinal wellbeing, respiratory framework, and heart wellbeing. The impact of needle therapy in improving vagal tone can likewise ensure against neurodegenerative ailments.

Muscle unwinding to oversee nervousness and increment vagal tone

One approach to improve vagus nerve work is to perform dynamic muscle unwinding. On examination including individuals under pressure, we found out that muscle unwinding brought down sentiments of stress and uneasiness. Unwinding treatment increments vagal action and gives various medical advantages. The expansion in vagal tone likewise brought down circulatory strain, decline cholesterol, and lower resting pulse. To perform dynamic muscle unwinding to animate your vagus nerve, start by straining the muscles in your feet and holding for 10 seconds, at that point discharging them. Rehash this for each muscle bunch as you stir your way up to your body. Do this for 20 minutes every day to profit by expanded vagus nerve incitement.

Polyvagal Hypothesis

Imagining cerebrum science can be something like envisioning a sea tempest. In spite of the fact that we can envision a terrible climate, it is hard to envision change in that climate. In any case, Stephen Porges' polyvagal hypothesis gives advisors a valuable image of the sensory system that can control us in our endeavors to support customers.

Porges' polyvagal hypothesis created out of his analyses with the vagus nerve. The vagus nerve serves the parasympathetic sensory system, which is the quieting part of our sensory system mechanics. The parasympathetic piece of the autonomic sensory system adjusts the thoughtful dynamic part, yet it is considerably more nuanced ways than we comprehended before polyvagal hypothesis.

Our three-section sensory system

Before the polyvagal hypothesis, our sensory system was envisioned as a two-section opposing framework, with more actuation flagging not so much quieting but rather more quieting flagging less enactment. Polyvagal hypothesis recognizes a third sensory system reaction usually called the social commitment framework. This is a perky blend of actuation and quieting that works out of extraordinary nerve impact.

The social commitment framework causes us to explore connections. Helping our customers move into the utilization of their social commitment framework enables them to turn out to be increasingly adaptable in their adapting styles. The two different pieces of our sensory system capacity to assist us with overseeing dangerous circumstances, most instructors are as of now acquainted with the two guard components activated by these two pieces of the sensory system: thoughtful battle or flight and parasympathetic shutdown, now and then called stop or black out. Utilization of our social commitment framework, then again, requires a feeling of wellbeing.

Polyvagal hypothesis encourages us to comprehend that the two parts of the vagus nerve quiet the body, yet they do as such in various manners. Shutdown, or stop or-black out, happens through the dorsal part of the vagus nerve. This response can feel like the exhausted muscles and tipsiness of terrible influenza. At the point when the dorsal vagal nerve closes down the body, it can move us into fixed status or separation. Notwithstanding, influencing the heart and lungs, the dorsal branch influences the body working beneath the stomach and is engaged with stomach related problems. The central part of the vagal nerve influences the body, working over the stomach. This branch serves the social commitment framework. The ventral vagal nerve hoses the body's routinely dynamic state. Picture controlling a pony as you ride it back to the stable. You would keep on pulling back on and discharge the reins in nuanced approaches to guarantee that the steed keeps up a proper speed. Moreover, the ventral vagal nerve permits enactment in a nuanced way, therefore, offering an unexpected quality in comparison to thoughtful actuation.

Ventral vagal discharge into movement takes milliseconds, though thoughtful initiation takes seconds and includes different compound responses that are much the same as losing the pony's reins. In addition, when the battle or flight substance responses have started, it can take our bodies 10–20 minutes to come back to our pre-battle/pre-flight state. Ventral vagal discharge into action doesn't include these sorts of concoction responses. Along these lines, we can make faster modifications between initiation and quieting, like what we can do when we utilize the reins to control the pony. On the off chance that you go to a canine park, you will see certain apprehensive pooches. They display battle or flight practices. Different mutts will flag a desire to play. This flagging frequently takes the structure that people capture for the descending confronting hound present in yoga. At the point when a canine gives this sign, it prompts a degree of excitement that can be exceptional. Nonetheless, this lively vitality has an altogether different soul than the force of battle or flight practices. This fun-loving soul describes the social commitment framework. At the point when we experience our condition as protected, we work from our social commitment framework.

Injury's impact on sensory system reaction

In the event that we have uncertain injury from before, we may live in a variant of unending battle or flight. We might have the option to channel this battle or flight tension into exercises. For example, cleaning the house, raking the forgets about or working at the recording center, yet these exercises will have an unexpected vibe in comparison they would on the off chance that they were finished with social commitment science (think "Whistle While You Work").

For some injury survivors, no movement effectively channels their battle or flight sensations. Therefore, they feel caught and their bodies shut down. These customers may live in a variant of the never-ending shutdown. A research focuses on the shutdown reaction through creature perceptions and bodywork with customers. A clarification requires a shiver or shakes to release suspended battle or-flight energy. In a perilous circumstance, on the off chance that we have shut down and an open door for dynamic endurance presents itself, we can wake ourselves up. As instructors, we may perceive this move from shutdown to battle or trip in a customer's move from misery into uneasiness.

However, how might we help our customers move into their social commitment science? On the off chance that customers live in an increasingly dissociative, discouraged, shutdown way, we should assist them with moving incidentally into battle or flight. As customers experience a battle or flight force, we should then assist them with finding a feeling of wellbeing. At the point when they can detect that they are protected, they can move into their social commitment framework.

The body-mindfulness procedures that are a piece of subjective conduct treatment (CBT) and argumentative conduct treatment (DBT) can assist customers with moving out of dissociative, shutdown reactions by urging them to turn out to be increasingly epitomized. At the point when customers are increasingly present in their bodies and better ready to take care of flitting solid pressure, they can wake up from a shutdown reaction. As customers enact out of shutdown and move toward battle or flight sensations, the idea rebuilding strategies that are additionally part of CBT and DBT can instruct customers to assess their wellbeing all the more precisely. Intelligent listening procedures can assist customers with feeling an association with their advisors. This makes it feasible for these customers to have a sense of security enough to move into social commitment science.

Explicit parts of ventral vagal nerve working

The name social commitment framework was picked because the ventral vagal nerve influences the center ear, which sifts through foundation commotions to make it simpler to hear the human voice. It additionally influences facial muscles and therefore the capacity to make open outward appearances. At long last, it influences the larynx and hence vocal tone and vocal designing, helping people make sounds that mitigate each other.

Polyvagal Theory

Autonomic sensory system is about wellbeing. This hypothesis offers exact science to seeing how the vagus nerve, one piece of this framework, which associates the mind, to the heart, to the viscera (the organs of the gut), identifies with our human capacity to interface and speak with one another. Finding out about the vagus nerve enables us to comprehend our sound human sensory system, and how it typically identifies with the upgrades it experiences as fluctuating degrees of security and threat.

This significant nerve is appropriately named by the Latin base of "vagus," which signifies "meander," in view of the broad association it has all through the body. Past speculations clarified that the parasympathetic sensory system, through the quieting impact of the vagus nerve, worked contrary to the thoughtful sensory system. The thoughtful sensory system empowers us for physical activity in the midst of hardship by expanding our pulse and circulatory strain, while all the while putting different capacities like the stomach related framework on hold. This framework empowers us to run from a perilous creature or to act rapidly to manage emergencies without halting and consider it.

The Autonomic Nervous System

This hypothesis gives us a progressively mind-boggling logical comprehension of a three-section various leveled model and how the vagus nerve is straightforwardly identified with a lucid arrangement of correspondence and association inside the autonomic framework.

The expression "neuroception" to allude to our inborn oblivious mindfulness through the autonomic sensory system to impacts in the body, in the earth, and in connections between individuals, at the end of the day, we distinguish perils before we have the opportunity to consider it. This enlightens us regarding the unpretentious feeling of security or risk that possibly influences any association on the planet The hypothesis depicts the autonomic sensory system has having three subdivisions that identify with social conduct and association. The most seasoned of these subdivisions is the "dorsal vagal," a piece of the parasympathetic sensory system that empowers us to close down, or "solidify" when a circumstance of risk feels wild and we are overpowered. The second is our thoughtful sensory system, or "battle/flight," framework. Furthermore, the most advanced and complex of the subdivisions is our mammalian parasympathetic social correspondence and social commitment framework – the ventral vagus. This is a mind-boggling system of quick, myelinated neural filaments beginning in the brainstem that directs our pulse, breathing, hearing, facial muscles, and vocalizing.

The hypothesis is progressive, implying that every one of the three of these subdivisions pursue a characteristic request contingent upon the perception of wellbeing or threat in the circumstance. In the event that nature is distinguished as sheltered, we are allowed to utilize the ventral vagal social commitment framework, which implies that we are moderately free to act naturally, express our very own emotions, utilize outward appearance effectively, and utilize a regulated voice design. Additionally, our pulse is generally quiet, we inhale unreservedly, and we sift through human language from foundation commotion. However, in the event that we are not recognizing the earth as protected, we fall into a battle or flight, endurance mode (this is the previously mentioned "thoughtful sensory system" dominating). Also, if that framework bombs as well, and we keep on feeling dangerous, we normally fall once again into the solidifying or closing down dorsal vagal mode. In these increasingly crude modes, a significant part of the previously mentioned limits is killed, leaving an individual with far less capacity to identify with the world socially.

Injury and the Polyvagal Theory

With regards to post-horrible pressure, these subdivisions are responding not just to the quick wellbeing or threat in their condition, but also to communication inside between the prompt condition and a feeling of activating action dependent on previous existence occasions. In this manner, in the event that somebody encountered an occasion in adolescence in which they didn't have a sense of security, an occasion in their present grown-up life may resound such an encounter within, and this individual may fall back on the cruder neural frameworks of intuitively expecting to fend off, escape, or shutdown so as to endure.

Every one of us encounters some level of injury in our initial lives.

Regardless of whether it was an occasion that brought an incredible dread or we felt a profound absence of help in a huge circumstance, or whether it was a progression of occasions that gave us dread perplexity, or a feeling of not being sheltered. Any of these encounters may have stayed in our sensory systems and develop to add dread to circumstances further down the road that helps our internal framework to remember the peril.

CHAPTER 3: Diseases and Disorders Associated with Vagus Nerve

There are different components inside our bodies with numerous capacities. Their performing multiple tasks functions keep us healthy, avoid ailment, and permit the body parts to cooperate consistently as one. One of these multitasks is the vagus nerve. You may have never known about it, however, this nerve plays out a few essential capacities. It is consistently at work. Regularly in the event that you are encountering things like tension, mind haze, weakness, gut issues, depersonalization, and weariness, it could possibly be an aftereffect of a vagus nerve issue.

It doesn't mean this nerve is out to hurt us. Despite what might be expected, it needs our bodies to keep up high usefulness measures. The issue comes whenever aggravated or harmed. In like manner, the vagus nerve turns into a reluctant quiet foe. Before going into the best ten issue of the vagus nerve however, we should discover increasingly about what it is. Very few individuals truly realize what the vagus nerve is, so first, let me clarify that. Being, the vagus nerve, the longest of cranial nerves in the body that manages the gut and therefore it influence the cardiovascular, resistant, endocrine, and respiratory frameworks. That implies it's an entirely significant nerve in the human body. Therefore, when that nerve is useless, you can envision it can have some entirely strange symptoms.

This past fall, I made sense of that my vagus nerve is, in one way or another broken. What's more, things being what they are, many individuals have a useless vagus nerve. At the point when you battle with vagus nerve brokenness, you can be fit as a fiddle for quite a while, contract a bug, or reach a stopping point, and afterward, your body will take a long time to recoup. I became so ill that I didn't have the vitality to try and get up for a considerable length of time and likely would have shriveled away if my mother didn't bring me nourishment. Living with vagus nerve brokenness is something that you need to figure out how to live in light of the fact that there is no fix. So on the off chance that you have a companion with a brokenness vagus nerve if it's not too much trouble attempt to get them and read through these basic side effects that accompany it.

Chronic nausea

Unfortunately, this implies there isn't a great deal that appears to be mouth-watering to eat. Since you are equipped with more information about the vagus nerve and its capacities, how about we plunge into the main issues it can cause. With such a great amount going on in the realm of this nerve, tragically, at times things separate. Vagus nerve brokenness prompts various side effects that many don't have the foggiest idea about the nerve is liable for.

Here are the best-related issues:

- Irritable Bowel Syndrome (IBS)
- Obesity and weight gain
- Chronic exhaustion
- Depression
- Bradycardia and tachycardia (Irregular heartbeat; too slow or quick individually)
- Peptic Ulcer
- Weight misfortune
- Gastroparesis
- Chronic aggravation
- Epilepsy

This one nerve can cause such a significant number of issues. You may be encountering a portion of its belongings and be totally unconscious of the underlying driver. Knowing a portion of the causes that can prompt vagus nerve issue, can help forestall these issues

What Causes Vagus Nerve Disorders?

Harm to the vagus nerve can be avoided now and again, while in others another infirmity or injury might be the reason. Providing engine nerve driving forces from the tongue and voice box muscles, just as getting tangible motivations from the chest and mid-region organs, ear, and throat is a difficult task. Add sending instinctive nerve heartbeats to the stomach and chest organ organs, and throat organs, and there is space for lamentable accidents en route. In that capacity, vagus nerve harm can be brought about by:

Constant Alcohol Abuse

Constant liquor misuse is a whole lot of nothing for the autonomic sensory system, as it has a poisonous, and portion related impact. Strikingly, the vagus nerve is one of those that can be hurtfully influenced by this kind of misuse. This maltreatment, known as alcoholic neuropathy, makes harm various nerves. Sadly, if a greater number of nerves than the vagus are influenced, side effects can be significantly progressively dangerous for the body's general working.

Diabetes

Predictable increment in glucose can prompt changed nerve science. As this infection can bring about nerve harm to a significant number of them, the vagus nerve doesn't getaway. Gastroparesis is one of the essential consequences of diabetes-prompted harm to the nerve. In like manner, side effects incorporate clogging, spewing, and stomach swell. Fundamentally, the stomach and digestive system muscles are never again ready to move appropriately nourishment around appropriately. Complexities during Surgeries

During medical procedures concentrated on the small digestive system or stomach, the vagus nerve can be harmed. One that is generally connected with this sort of harm is the laparoscopic hemifundoplication. In this manner, this method is utilized as a treatment for gastric reflux.

Diseases

Upper respiratory viral diseases infer another offender as it identifies with vagus nerve harm. Obviously, it may be difficult to bind if there has been harm at first, as side effects appear to be a standard cold or gentle influenza. Conceivably, they incorporate nasal clog, runny nose, and hack. Obviously, it becomes clearer that there might be vagus harm when side effects stay for the long stretch. Subsequently, should vagus nerve harm be the reason, it is spoken to as viral vagal neuropathy or PVVN.

Apparently, a few people experience the ill effects of issues talking appropriately, such as throat clearing, vocal weariness, and diligent hack. As we plunge further into the universe of the vagus nerve, it tends to be somewhat startling thinking about the manners in which it tends to be influenced. Consecutively, the uplifting news that we bring means a few different ways to treat the clutters and turn around the harm.

How to Stimulate the Vagus Nerve?

A similar way the vagus nerve invigorates such a large number of components inside our bodies, is the same way it needs some as well. In addition, this keeps the nerve appropriately working and ready to play out its assignments. In extreme cases, a gadget can be embedded under the skin and takes into consideration incitement utilizing electrical heartbeats. Furthermore, the manner in which it works makes this gadget much like a cardiovascular pacemaker. Besides, accomplishing vagus nerve incitement comes significantly before an issue emerges. Then again, it occurs if pressure or harm shows up before existing manifestations deteriorate. Indisputably, a large number of these energizers include things we can undoubtedly utilize in our day-by-day lives. Some may even amaze you.

Methods for vagus nerve incitement:

- Yoga and Meditation - both of these things increment parasympathetic framework movement. Attempt a couple "Oms" the vagus nerve adores it.
- Breathing gradually and profoundly from your stomach
- Exercise-The gut stream is invigorated by mellow exercise.
- Oxytocin
- Positive social associations
- Fasting
- Letting your body conform to cold - cold water in the face, cold showers, and so on
- Acupuncture
- Zinc
- Gargling - gets the muscles at the back of the throat which helps in incitement.
- Massage
- Probiotics - more proof identified with gut microbiota having impacts on the mind.
- Chanting or Singing
- Laughter - can truly be the best prescription.
- Eating Fiber
- Laying on your correct side when dozing

Likely, the rundown comes as a broad one with the end goal that it controls your day-by-day exercises. It additionally incorporates rehearses like straining stomach muscles or hacking, rehearsing Tai Chi which expands pulse and getting some sun. Eventually, the simple things that we do each day and presumably don't understand, appear to have a huge effect on our vagus nerve.

Medications for Vagus Nerve Disorders

If you accept that your vagus nerve isn't responding to boosts the manner in which it should, at that point your initial step ought to be to get the counsel of your normal specialist. They can prescribe you to a nerve expert that will have the option to decide if you are experiencing a nerve issue.

Experience nerve treatment

If it is resolved that your vagus nerve isn't working appropriately, at that point you should experience nerve treatment. Treatment normally incorporates vagus nerve incitement. A gadget will be connected to the nerve to send electric heartbeats to the nerve to help manage the sign sent by the nerve, this gadget are in capacities comparable to a pacemaker in the heart.

Therapeutic treatment

Notwithstanding, treating the nerve, the individuals who are experiencing this issue should look out for restorative treatment to help manage the reactions that this condition has caused on the body. A conventional pacemaker might be expected to help guarantee that the heart pulsates routinely and prescription is expected to help ensure that your stomach related framework is controlled appropriately.

Chronic illnesses and inflammation

Incendiary reactions assume a focal job in the advancement and industriousness of numerous infections and can prompt incapacitating constant torment. Much of the time, aggravation is your body's reaction to push. Hence, diminishing "battle or flight" reactions in the sensory system and bringing down organic markers for stress can likewise decrease irritation. Regularly, specialists recommend drugs to battle irritation. Nonetheless, there is developing proof that another method to battle aggravation is by drawing in the vagus nerve and improving "vagal tone." This can be accomplished through every day propensities, for example, yoga, and contemplation or in increasingly outrageous instances of irritation, for example, rheumatoid joint pain (RA) - by utilizing an embedded gadget for vagus nerve incitement (VNS).

The vagus nerve is known as the "meandering nerve" since it has numerous branches that veer from two thick stems established in the cerebellum and brainstem that meander to the least viscera of your belly, contacting your heart, and most significant organs en route. Vagus signifies "meandering" in Latin. The words drifter, dubious, and transient are altogether gotten from a similar Latin root.

In early 20s of last century, a German physiologist named Otto Loewi found that invigorating the vagus nerve caused a decrease in pulse by setting off the arrival of a substance he coined Vagusstoff (German for "Vagus Substance"). The "vagus substance" was later recognized as acetylcholine and turned it into the main synapse at any point distinguished by researchers. Vagusstoff (acetylcholine) resembles a sedative that you can self-direct, just by taking a couple of full breaths with long breathes out. Intentionally taking advantage of the intensity of your vagus nerve can make a condition of quiet inward while subduing your irritation reflex. The vagus nerve is the prime part of the parasympathetic sensory system which controls the "rest-and-digest" or "tend-and-become a close acquaintance with" reactions. On the other side, to look after homeostasis, the thoughtful sensory system drives the "battle or flight" reaction.

Healthy Vagal Tone Is the Key Factor of a Feedback Circle Strictly Connected to Positive Emotions

Solid vagal tone is shown by a slight increment of the pulse when you breathe in and a decline of pulse when you breathe out. Profound diaphragmatic breathing - with a long, slow breathe out - is critical to animating the vagus nerve and easing back pulse and circulatory strain, particularly in the midst of execution uneasiness. A higher vagal tone list is connected to physical and mental prosperity. On the other hand, a low vagal tone list is related to irritation, wretchedness, negative mindsets, depression, respiratory failures, and stroke.

Their exploration recommends that positive feelings, vigorous social associations, and physical wellbeing impact each other in a self-supporting upward winding dynamic and criticism circle that researchers are simply starting to comprehend.

Most researchers utilized a Loving-Kindness Meditation (LKM) procedure, in order to assist members with getting better at self-producing positive feelings. Notwithstanding, they additionally found that essentially considering positive social associations and attempting to improve affectionate human bonds likewise caused upgrades in vagal tone.

How Does the Vagus Nerve Convey Gut Instincts to the Brain? Depended on discoveries by analysts in Switzerland who recognized how the vagus nerve passes on "hunches" of nervousness and dread to the cerebrum, Clinical, and exploratory examinations show that pressure and gloom are related with the up-guideline of the safe framework, including expanded creation of genius incendiary cytokines. When managed to patients or research center creatures, cytokines have been found to instigate run of the mill indications of melancholy. Along these lines, a few instances of low mind-set, low vitality, and absence of inspiration might be because of raised degrees of cytokine proteins. As of late, a universal group of specialists from Amsterdam and the United States directed a clinical preliminary, which shows that animating the vagus nerve with a little embedded gadget essentially diminished aggravation and improved results for patients with rheumatoid joint inflammation by hindering cytokine creation.

RA is a constant "Incendiary Ailment" that influences roughly 1.3 million individuals in the United States and costs several billions of dollars to treat every year, as per the scientists. The neuroscientists and immunology specialists associated with this examination utilized the innovative innovation to outline neural hardware that controls irritation. In one circuit - named "the fiery reflex" - activity possibilities transmitted in the vagus nerve repress the creation of genius incendiary cytokines.

This is the main human investigation intended to diminish indications of rheumatoid joint pain by invigorating the vagus nerve with a little embedded gadget, which set off a chain response that decreased cytokine levels and aggravation. Despite the fact that this investigation concentrated on rheumatoid joint pain, the preliminary's outcomes may have suggestions for patients experiencing other incendiary ailments, including Parkinson's, Crohn, and Alzheimer's.

We can therefore state without doubts that the main investigation to assess in the case of invigorating the fiery reflex legitimately with an embedded electronic gadget can treat RA in people. We have recently indicated that focusing on the provocative reflex may decrease aggravation in creature models and in vitro models of RA . . ., which may be pertinent for other resistant intervened provocative infections also.

These discoveries recommend another way to deal with battling maladies that are at present treated with generally costly medications that have a large group of symptoms. VNS gives medicinal services supplies a conceivably progressively successful approach to improve the lives of individuals experiencing interminable incendiary illnesses.

CHAPTER 4: Vagus Nerve and Social Engagement

Our Autonomic Nervous System (ANS), is the director of the internal symphony in our body, liable for the control of our real capacities not intentionally coordinated, for example, breathing, the heartbeat, pulse, perspiring, and stomach related procedures. The ANS is continually murmuring at a specific beat, and how well it works, decides our physical, mental, and enthusiastic wellbeing.

The Social Engagement System

The Vagus Nerve is related to increments in wellbeing and passionate prosperity as it produces positive conditions of unwinding and social commitment. Our Social Engagement framework is working ideally when we have a sense of security and associate with the world and others. For the duration of the day, we always get signs and triggers through our faculties and sash, which acts as a second sensory system. We have an outer situation, which is the outside world, yet we additionally have an inward domain, which is the physiology of our body, such as jumping into a remote ocean, so much is occurring underneath the surface, and wave after wave.

Our intuitive inside sifting framework will promptly assess whether we are sheltered or need to make a move. This occurs without us in any event, monitoring it, or contemplating it. At the point when we have a sense of security, we can unwind, grow, go ahead, and step out into the world. When there is pressure or apparent risk in our psyches, we depend on our social commitment framework to set up a feeling of wellbeing and association. This can be accomplished through a discussion, a call for help, looking, or hearing a quieting voice. This will send flags down to our hearts and lungs, hindering our pulse and extending our relaxing. It especially works as a foot brake - a Vagal Brake - and has a quieting and alleviating impact on our sensory system.

Picture the inverse: For instance, an individual says something to you that makes you feel upset. What occurs? We will in general change our outward appearance flagging our agitated, the tone of our voice changes frequently to an angrier, stronger, or higher pitch, we look for approval, and we get the telephone and converse with somebody. On the off chance that the social commitment framework neglects to determine the pressure and it stays dynamic in our body, at that point we will naturally turn to the more established organic reaction, one stage down the stepping stool into battle/flight, with the Sympathetic Nervous framework kicking in.

What are the zones innervated by the Ventral Vagus Nerve?

The Ventral Vagus Nerve innervates the territories over the stomach: face, throat, voice box, larynx, center ear, heart, lungs and serves the social commitment framework. This framework is managed by 5 cranial nerves and when these nerves work well, we can appreciate ideal physical and enthusiastic wellbeing including extraordinary companionship, backing, holding, and adoring connections. At the point when we are socially drawn in, we can be inventive, positive, gainful, and upbeat. Socially connected which implies we are free from dangers, peril, superfluous stresses, and now in great physical wellbeing. The Social Engagement System guides us in direction, correspondence, and outward appearance and involves the accompanying cranial nerves, which all begin in the brainstem.

- 5th Cranial Nerve: this is the Trigeminal Nerve: it is the face and jaw biting muscles.
- 7th Cranial Nerve: this is the Facial Nerve: it controls hearing,

center ear, and every facial muscle for informative outward appearances and copy. Neural guideline for the center ear muscles
- 9th Cranial Nerve: this is Glossopharyngeal Nerve: it controls the Tongue, Throat, and Swallowing. It is answerable for sounds delivered by the Voicebox, vocal tone, and making sounds.
- 10th Cranial Nerve: this is the Ventral Vagus Nerve branch. It innervates little muscles in the throat and salivation.
- 11th Cranial Nerve: it innervates the Trapezius and Sternocleidomastoid (SCM) muscles in the neck for head and neck development, direction, and having the option to turn your head.

Practices we show when socially engaged:

- We have a sense of security
- We are associated with ourselves and to other people,
- We can be close
- We contact an associate with others, we can bond
- We are quiet, inhale effectively, and we can think unmistakably
- Muscles are loose
- We feel fun-loving, we move, sing and tummy chuckle
- We feel love and can really cherish
- We can really unwind and unwind into association with others
- Feel the world: it is wide, and we are one with the surroundings

Side effects we can have when not socially locked in:

- We feel on edge or are not ready to unwind around ourselves as well as other people
- We feel shut down or discouraged
- We are overpowered
- We feel outraged, nauseate, disgrace
- We habitually need to do things
- We are wired
- We are antisocial people - don't generally draw in and escape the

world
- What do you do? If you don't mind fill in your very own interesting thing you do when you are not socially locked in.

Craniosacral Therapy

The craniosacral system comprises of the film encompassing the spinal string, spinal liquid, the spinal string sac, and the mind. Alongside the focal sensory system, this framework is the most significant framework contained inside the human body. The spinal rope and the cerebrum contained inside this framework, impact, and help control the focal sensory system. The two frameworks together control body development, perception, thinking, feelings, and wellbeing. In the event that there is a glitch in this framework, the wellbeing of the whole body is in peril.

The spinal liquid that is contained inside the film, known as the meninges, beats at a particular cadence for every individual. As a rule, this spinal liquid heartbeat rate is around ten heartbeats for each moment. This craniosacral beat is like circulatory strain, in that it beats as it moves, both all through the spinal string. Any kind of damage can make pressure be put on the liquid and can interfere with the equalization of the spinal liquid stream. Whenever the liquid is blocked or can't beat accurately, medical issues are framed. Weight put on the spinal liquid can influence the whole body and cause hurts, torments, issues concentrating, limited development, and different issues, for example, migraines, ceaseless exhaustion disorder, fibromyalgia, scoliosis, and other connective tissue and joint sicknesses.

What is craniosacral therapy?

Most researchers structured craniosacral treatment during the 1970s. He put together his way to deal with recuperation, with respect to standards and hypotheses made by some researchers, who was a rehearsing osteopath during the 1900s. Dr. Upledger went through years rehearsing and consummating his system. Upledger, a biomechanics teacher at

Michigan State University, held great and several clinical preliminaries as he dealt with this new method for recuperating. The rule behind CST is the information on how the spinal framework functions and how the power behind the recuperating functions likewise. Regular stressors can affect the weight of the spinal liquid, just as mishaps and damage. By utilizing a light touch, experts of CST can frequently get the liquids streaming and beating in an ordinary way, in this manner facilitating the torments that a blocked stream can cause.

Likewise, CST can discharge pressures and stressors that are contained in the tissues encompassing the framework. This thusly helps in keeping up with the spinal and cerebrum framework; however, it can likewise work to fix the focal sensory system. By normalizing the beats and the rhythms of the cerebrospinal liquid around the spine and the cerebrum, dysfunctions of the body, for example, incessant agony, strokes, neurological hindrances, and sports wounds can be both reduced and restored.

What are Craniosacral Therapy Benefits?

Craniosacral treatment benefits incorporate diminishing the accompanying issue and issues such as:

- Headaches and Chronic headaches
- Chronic neck torment
- Upper and lower-back agony
- Stress and pressure
- Chronic weariness disorder
- Fibromyalgia
- Post-horrendous pressure disorder
- Orthopedic issues
- Arthritis
- TMJ

Moreover, a great people discover that the treatment is incredibly unwinding. Numerous individuals will in general float off to rest during their treatment. This is in reality exceptionally helpful, in light of the fact that a casual body reacts better to remedial recuperating.

Different advantages incorporate the impact it has on the connective tissues of the body. These connective tissues cannot just apply outrageous weight on the muscles, but they likewise can restrain movement. Since they are not ready to be seen on most analytic pictures, the manifestations an individual displays can frequently appear to be strange and are regularly rejected by conventional therapeutic professionals. Another part of CST is Somato-Emotional Release, which holds that feelings are additionally part of a bodily injury and that by discharging the horrible feelings, mending is quicker and progressively successful. Regularly, the back rub systems utilized in the CST discharges these feelings. Other treatment benefits incorporate mindfulness of the body and the arrival of the body's oblivious recuperating capacities.

Normally, the customer or patient rests completely dressed on an agreeable couch or unique remedial table. The Craniosacral Therapist at that point tenderly lays their hands on the patient. Most of the craniosacral advisors are osteopaths, chiropractors, rub specialists, or physical advisors. Subsequent to getting a full restorative history from the customer, the advisor at that point starts with the feet, and utilizing a lightweight, close to the weight applied by a coin being set on the skin, the specialist starts to stir their way up the body of the patient. For the most part, the advisor begins with the feet and works upwards. Notwithstanding, utilizing CST, applied kinesiology is likewise used to help with the reflexive methodology.

CST is a comprehensive treatment, since it attempts to avoid and fix ailment and malady by utilizing the body in general. Specialists who practice CST are commonly delicate professionals who tune in to their patients.

CHAPTER 5: Tapping into the Power of the Vagus Nerve

Did you realize that constant pressure undermines your conduct when seeing someone? Applied neuroscience explore shows that when your mind and the sensory system are commanded by the pressure reaction, you are inclined to a more noteworthy nervousness, crabbiness, negative state of mind and conduct unbending nature.

This is because when focused on, you lose access to higher subjective capacities like focusing, tuning in, arranging, thinking, and the ability to impart adequately. Did you additionally realize that you have the ability to diminish worry in a moment? It's valid. You can change your experience by changing your breath. Here's the reason.

The Autonomic Nervous System (ANS)

The autonomic sensory or nervous system (ANS), a key player in the battle, flight, or stop reaction, has for quite some time been proposed to impact social conduct, its capacity is to react to ecological requests by either catalyzing the mind-body framework in light of the danger or keeping up homeostatic equalization during which rest, fix, and development are conceivable. The ANS is isolated into two significant branches: the thoughtful sensory nervous system (SNS) and the parasympathetic sensory system (PNS). The SNS is frequently likened to a physiological "gas pedal." When a creature sees risk, the SNS dumps a course of stress hormones into the circulation system that expansion pulse, circulatory strain, and breath, contract muscle, and discourage all unimportant capacities like processing.

In this express, the mind's dread hardware, which dwells in the limbic framework, is likewise predominant, drawing significant assets from the prefrontal cortex and different areas of the cerebrum where arranging, thinking and powerful correspondence happen. At the point when the SNS is predominant, social conduct gets constrained to endurance techniques, for example, animosity, shirking, or withdrawal.

The offset to the SNS, the PNS, is regularly thought of as a physiological "brake pedal." Under state of wellbeing, the PNS starts an unwinding reaction, which discourages pulse, circulatory strain, and breath lessens muscle tone/compression and enables the living being to take part in reparative and helpful capacities, an example is in absorption. In this express, the cerebrum's dread hardware is never again activated, opening up higher request subjective working and empowering a more extensive and increasingly adaptable scope of conduct.

The Vagus Nerve

Despite the fact that the SNS and PNS contribute fundamentally to our social collection, theory recommends that, for well-evolved creatures and people, the connection between ANS working and conduct is unquestionably progressively unpredictable. Contemporary neuroscientists and clinical analysts are starting to observe the significant impact of the Xth cranial nerve, otherwise called the vagus nerve, in the improvement and upkeep of versatile and maladaptive social conduct.

Charles Darwin previously noticed the vagus nerve and its job in social conduct in 1872. In his book, The Expression of Emotions in Man and Animals, Darwin recommended that the focal sensory system and the vagus nerve take part in a dynamic, proportional trade of neurologic data that influences the unconstrained articulation of feeling. Darwin battled that human emotional articulation is fundamental to endurance, adjustment, and normal determination. As opposed to being essentially a response to encounter, Darwin conjectured that passionate articulation is proportionally connected to physiology and that particular neural pathways bi-directionally trade data between cerebrum structures and major instinctive organs, for example, the heart, lungs, and gut.

"At the point when the heart is influenced, it responds on the cerebrum," composed Darwin; "and the condition of the mind again responds through the pneumogastric (vagus) nerve on the heart; so that under any fervor there will be a lot of common activity and response between these, the two most significant organs of the body" (Darwin, 1872, P69). This is maybe one of the principal Western logical affirmations of the mind-body association! The word, vagus, is Latin for drifter. In fact, the impact of the vagus nerve is diffuse. It starts in the medulla oblongata, in the mind stem, and ventures to numerous instinctive organs including the heart, lungs, and stomach related tract, autonomously of the spinal segment. The vagal framework speaks to a complex of nerve branches that hand-off sign from the mind to the body (afferent) and from instinctive organs to the cerebrum (efferent). This bi-directional impact takes into account the productive guideline of metabolic yield because of ecological requests. Action of the vagus nerve is alluded to as vagal tone and estimated opposite respiratory sinus arrhythmia (RSA). RSA alludes to the musical increment and decline in a pulse that happens synchronously with relaxing. During inward breath, our pulse increments (thoughtful sensory system impact) and vagal impact diminish.

During exhalation, be that as it may, pulse diminishes as vagus impact builds (parasympathetic sensory system impact). RSA, as a pointer of vagal tone is utilized to look at the utilitarian condition of the parasympathetic sensory system. In particular, the several number of RSA changeability gives a proportion of the impact of the vagus nerve on the heart. More elevated levels of RSA changeability demonstrate more noteworthy vagal tone during the breath cycle, which additionally mirrors the body's capacity to react to expanding metabolic requests and ecological difficulties. The view of genuine or envisioned danger enacts the SNS and discourages PNS, or vagal impact. These planned physical responses increment metabolic yield because of ecological requests. When danger is expelled, the vagus becomes predominant and enhances vagal tone increments, starting the instinctive organs' arrival to homeostasis during which recuperation, development, and fixation continues. Stress, at that point, is any genuine or envisioned improvement that upsets homeostasis and prompts the withdrawal of PNS/vagal tone and the inception of a fast SNS reaction.

The main stage, which we find in crude living things, is related to immobilization practices, for example, solidifying and faking demise within the sight of danger. The subsequent stage incorporates SNS impact, which increments metabolic yield and restrains PNS/vagal tone to activate for battle or flight. The third stage, which is one of a kind to warm-blooded creatures, incorporates the expansion of myelinated vagal nerves that are able to do quickly managing heart yield to encourage both commitment and separation from ecological stimuli. This myelinated part of the vagal framework controls facial muscles relating to talking, gulping, sucking and, in particular, relaxing. It additionally controls SNS pathways to the heart, and can quickly start unwinding quietly. These administrative frameworks of the vagus and related cranial nerves are accepted to give the substrate to passionate encounters and social conduct. Polyvagal hypothesis interfaces the development of the autonomic sensory system to passionate experience and articulation of vocal correspondence and social conduct. In his times of research, looking at the manners by which the phylogenic advancement of the vagus has influenced human conduct articulation, Porges found out that the more as of late developed, myelinated parts of the vagus nerve found in vertebrates assume a particular job in consideration, self-guideline, correspondence, enthusiastic articulation, versatility to stretch in different limits integral to social working. These myelinated vagus filaments, which send a sign to the mind significantly more rapidly than the phylogenetically more established, unmyelinated strands, hinder these more established frameworks. Thus the more up to date, myelinated vagal framework in vertebrates can supersede the sign of the SNS, a wonder that Porges alludes to as the vagal brake.

The Vagal Brake and Social Behavior

The vagal brake's fundamental capacity is to direct pulse through the fast hindrance and disinhibition of vagal tone to the heart. At the point when the brake is applied, vagal tone increments and cardiovascular yield is decreased advancing unwinding, self-calming, development, and fix. Then again, when the brake is discharged, the SNS gets predominant, and pulse increments to catalyze the framework in light of ecological requests. At the point when this brake is disabled in any way, shape or form, phylogenetically more seasoned autonomic reactions are initiated, bringing about a limited collection of battle or flight practices. As indicated by defenders of the polyvagal hypothesis, the vagal brake assumes a significant job in the advancement of fitting social conduct. In view of its ability to quickly discourage or enroll the SNS because of ecological requests, the brake considers prompt commitment and separation from others during social cooperation. In various investigations with babies and little youngsters, thinks about the show that vagal tone is a significant pointer of self-guideline, continued consideration, versatility and the capacity to quiet down subsequent to encountering a stressor. This ability to control conduct is a fundamentally significant capacity seeing someone. The individuals who can think and act deftly, keep up attentional control, and manage feelings and practices are unquestionably progressively ready to react properly to relational stressors and requests than the individuals who come up short on these capabilities.

Connecting the Vagus, Breath and Social Behavior

The vagus nerve is bi-directionally impacted, both in sending and accepting signs between the mind and instinctive organs. At the point when the body encounters physical or mental pressure, the vagus is selected in the inception of a compensatory conduct reaction by either applying or discharging the vagal brake. Yet, when genuine pressure is ceaseless, homeostatic equalization is troublesome if certainly feasible. The SNS turns out to be reliably predominant and the vagal brake is less every now and again applied.

The vagus nerve controls muscles related to talking, gulping, sucking and, above all, relaxing. It is characteristically connected to social conduct through its enactment of the muscles of the face and neck including those that affect outward appearance and vocal reverberation. Higher conditions of vagal tone and the ability to adequately utilize the vagal brake are connected to more noteworthy enthusiastic dependability, intellectual adaptability, conduct guideline, prosody of discourse, and suitable outward appearance - every single key limit of socially talented conduct. On the other hand, poor vagal brake guideline is connected to broken conduct. Notwithstanding its effect on facial muscles, the vagus, the two controls, and is impacted by breath. At the point when the vagal brake is actuated and the PNS framework is enlisted, heart and breath rates lower, and the framework comes back to a homeostatic state, which is normally experienced as unwinding. On the other hand, when the brake is lifted and the SNS overwhelms, breath and pulse become fast, and endurance situated practices identified with the battle or flight reaction become premier.

Since the vagal tone the two impacts and are affected by breath, we can increment vagal tone through control of the breath. As you will review that, there's vagal tone increment during exhalation. By hindering our breath through profound, purposeful breathing and lengthening our exhalation, we can initiate the vagal brake and inspire the unwinding reaction very quickly.

When this reaction starts and PNS is predominant, our minds stop to be administered by the limbic framework and dread hardware that constrains our ability to viably think, plan, reason and react to other people.

This implies that we are never again dependent upon a tight scope of protective or getaway practices. Through purposefully extending the breath and dragging out exhalation, we get to the unwinding reaction, but additionally the ability to be carefully present in relationship.

With time and practice, purposeful breathing can be utilized as an amazing asset to diffuse pressure and oversee troublesome or conflictual relational conditions.

Through changing of the body by means of the breath, we have the ability to change our outlook, yet additionally our relationship to other people.

CHAPTER 6: Exercise and Stimulation

We learnt so far

Being the biggest nerve in the body, the vagus nerve influences something other than the body's physical capacities. Some exploration shows that a sound vagus nerve is imperative to social holding and sympathy, just as our capacity to settle on complex choices. Spiritualists accept that it is additionally the convergence between our cognizant and oblivious personalities, the physical, and the unobtrusive bodies. Consequently, the vagus nerve might be the most applicable piece of our physical body that identifies with our true serenity and bliss.

Obviously, the vagus nerve assumes a basic job in our bodies; henceforth it is additionally crucial to our prosperity. Individuals with hindered vagal movement can experience the ill effects of discouragement, alarm issue, nervousness, state of mind swings and constant exhaustion. Physically, vagal unevenness can bring about peevish inside disorder, heftiness, heart consume, undesirable pulse, and ceaseless aggravation. Researchers have been leading examination on the vagus nerve to see how it influences our general prosperity. In their exploration, they found that invigorating the vagus nerve with the electrical sign has the potential for diminishing despondency and uneasiness. Researchers likewise found out that vagus nerve incitement can improve conditions, for example, epilepsy, and heftiness.

Vagus Nerve Stimulation Exercises

Individuals with ideal vagal tone are strong under pressure since they can undoubtedly move from an energized state to a casual state. This switches on the parasympathetic sensory system, which is liable for rest, assimilation, and richness. Subsequently, these people frequently appreciate superb absorption, ideal pulse, and great by and large wellbeing.

Tragically, it isn't in every case simple for somebody to turn on the parasympathetic sensory system and unwind. That is because we invest such a large amount of our energy in a condition of battle or flight. This state is represented by our thoughtful sensory system, which floods the body with pressure hormones. Fortunately, there are many regular and non-nosy ways that you can invigorate the vagus nerve. Here are five vagus nerve incitement activities to assist you with improving your vagal tone.

Careful Breathing

Long, profound breathing is the ideal approach to enact the vagus nerve. Despite the fact that the vagus nerve is as of now engaged with our automatic breathing, when we do it intentionally it improves vagal tone. This, thusly, allows the body to restore.

Here is a straightforward careful breathing activity. In the first place, try to sit serenely in a seat or on a collapsed cover. At that point, pursue this breath design:

- Sit upstanding and close the eyes
- As you breathe in, lift your collarbone and sit straighter
- As you breathe out, mollify and unwind
- As you breathe in, extend the sides of your rib confine
- As you breathe out, mellow and unwind
- As you breathe in, grow the front and back of your rib confine
- As you breathe out, mollify and unwind
- Repeat for 5-10 minutes.

Notwithstanding careful breathing, therapeutic yoga is a perfect method to invigorate the vagus nerve, as it fuses both the breath and loosening up stances. Here are three valuable helpful stances.

Upheld Forward Fold

Sit with legs expanded straight, and overlay forward over legs. Keep neck and shoulders loose. Make a point to help the middle/arms/head with a seat, reinforces or pads. On the off chance that the low back isn't happy, sit on a pad or collapsed cover. Hold for 10-15 minutes, breathing carefully.

Upheld Bridge

Lay level on the ground with legs twisted. Spot feet level on the ground, hips' width separated. Lift hips, and spot a square (or enormous book) under the low back/pelvis. Rest down onto the square. Hold for 10-15 minutes, breathing carefully.

Leaned back Spinal Twist with Bent Knees

Lay level on the ground with legs bowed. Spot feet level on the ground, and hold a square between the knees. Spread arms out in a T position. Take twisted knees over to the other side. Spot another square, reinforce, or collapsed cover underneath the knees in the event that they don't rest easily to the ground. Dismiss head from the knees. Hold 5-10 minutes, breathing carefully. At that point, rehash on the opposite side.

Exercising Meditation

Exercising Meditation is an awesome practice since you can do it anywhere and whenever. It includes very pondering considering doing a progression of activities that you ordinarily do naturally. To begin with, locate a decent area where you can stroll back and forth for 10-15 paces, or where you can walk consistently for 10-15 minutes. Stroll at whatever paces you'd like, separating each progression as pursues:

- Lift one foot thoroughly off the ground.
- Observe the foot as it swings forward and brings down.
- Observe the foot as it reaches the ground, impact point first.
- Feel the weight move onto that foot as the body pushes ahead.
- Continue for 10-15 minutes, breathing carefully.

Meditation - Mindfulness

The Vagus Nerve and meditation are entwined. The Vagus Nerve generally interpreted signifies "meandering nerve." It goes from the mind stem down to the midriff and associates with many significant organs taking an interest in a large number of our real capacities, for example, breathing, assimilation, pulse, and some more. It is personally associated with the parasympathetic part of the autonomic (automatic) sensory system and along these lines assumes a major job in controlling pressure. The autonomic sensory system runs through our bodies naturally without us taking an interest. Capacities, for example, pulse are a component of the autonomic sensory system.

The autonomic sensory system has two branches, the thoughtful, and the parasympathetic. The thoughtful branch is liable for placing us in battle or flight and the parasympathetic branch is answerable for removing us from battle or flight and managing our bodies when not engaged with a battle or flight occasion. Feelings of anxiety are noteworthy highs, and one reason for that is the marvel of stalling out in battle or flight. For various reasons our sensory systems are stalling out in the thoughtful mode implying that, the progressions that occur in our body/mind during battle or flight are not being settled after the occasion occurs. Subsequently those changes, to fluctuating degrees, remain with us for expanded timeframes. This results in constant pressure, which prompts a large group of physical, mental, and passionate side effects.

Science has given us various apparatuses whereby we can quantify different real capacities to decide feelings of anxiety. One of the best approaches to gauge these feelings of anxiety is by considering the Vagus Nerve incitement. At the point when the Vagus Nerve gets invigorated it affects the parasympathetic part of the autonomic sensory system to leave battle or flight in this manner decreasing pressure. Here's the manner by which that occurs through reflection. We realize that contemplation, especially care meditation (full regard for the present minute) is powerful in bringing down pressure. Care contemplation is the most examined way to deal with reflection having more than 2500 examinations distributed worldwide with a normal of 200 more for each month being distributed. I believe it to be the center point of the reflection wheel in that it upgrades the various contemplation draws near and can be an independent practice itself. These investigations showed that reflection could build vitality, lessen pressure, slow breathing, decline nervousness, diminish torment, increment bloodstream, and give a feeling of harmony to give some examples.

At the point when the Vagus Nerve gets the sign from these contemplation impacts, it makes an impression on the mind that everything is great, that there is no risk and there is no should be in battle or flight. The cerebrum at that point sends the message to the autonomic sensory system, which invigorates the parasympathetic branch to leave battle or flight and direct the frameworks into balance. This is a case of the Vagus Nerve and the mind cooperating. The mind can send messages to the body and the body to the cerebrum through the Vagus Nerve. It is intriguing to take note that an element of the body recently thought to run consequently, can in truth be affected deliberately through contemplation. This is significant and it gives us knowledge into the probability of numerous ways that we can deliberately partake in our wellbeing and its prosperity. This is again showing the psyche or body association, and how our contemplations, feelings, and physical sensations are interconnected, and how reflection can aid the smooth running of the framework.In the event that conceivable, practice your strolling contemplation shoeless. This enables you to see extra sensations as your feet contact the ground.

Yoga and Tai Chi

The vagus nerve can likewise be conditioned and fortified like a muscle, for instance: Massage and back rub oil, knead benefits for vagus nerve, quieting battle or flight reaction, yoga, and the vagus nerve Back rub: You can invigorate your vagus nerve by rubbing your feet and your neck along the carotid sinus, situated along the carotid courses on either side of your neck. The neck, back and shoulder back rub; or foot back rub can help bring down your pulse and circulatory strain.

Yoga and Tai Chi: Both yoga and kendo increment vagus nerve action and your parasympathetic framework when all is said and done. Studies have indicated that yoga builds GABA, a quieting synapse in your mind. Specialists trust it does this by animating vagal afferents (strands), which increment movement in the parasympathetic sensory system. This is particularly useful for the individuals who battle with tension or discouragement.

Breathing Slowly:

Your heart and neck contain neural receptors called baroreceptors, which identify the circulatory strain and transmit the neuronal sign to your mind. This initiates your vagus nerve, which interfaces with your heart to bring down circulatory strain and pulse. Slow breathing, with a generic equivalent measure of time taking in and out, expands the affectability of baroreceptors and vagal actuation.

The Amygdala

The amygdala is an almond-formed structure situated inside the foremost part of the worldly flaps. It is a segment of the limbic system and known to have an impact in controlling feeling, inspiration, and memory. It resembles a library, putting away the passionate recognitions that happen each time an idea enters our cerebrum. As such, every time we fabricate a memory, we initiate feelings, so we feel our body's response to our musings. The mind's main responsibility is to foresee and control results.

This implies past encounters, direct responses to recent developments, and structure rehash designs. The cerebrum is one-sided toward what it knows, and will pursue the easiest course of action. The amygdala recollects the emotions around every one of these picked ways, which are the Amygdala, vagus nerve, yoga life systems, yoga, and vagus nerve, feelings, and memory, yoga, and amygdala The amygdala enacts the battle or flight reactions with an expanded pulse and circulatory strain and invigorates the arrival of specific hormones. It gives programmed, fast, and oblivious response to musings or occasions.

The amygdala enacts at whatever point we experience anything through our faculties that helps us to remember the past injury. In this way, the best approach to manage current triggers is to return to the point of the injury, get to the put-away feeling, and discharge it from the body. The amygdala will never again feel an abundance feeling around that occasion, and it will never again be a trigger certain conduct later on.

Hyperactive vigilance is the point at which the amygdala is trapped on top of it of seeing a danger to life and reacting to it. Similarly as with the vagus nerve, we can utilize knead, slow breathing, and yoga practice to reset the framework.

Obviously, this is nevertheless a concise outline of complex frameworks, able to do more than which is portrayed here, and interconnected with different organs, and frameworks in the body. Be that as it may, I trust this has given somewhat more knowledge and comprehension into maybe how and why you respond to specific circumstances.

CHAPTER 7: Diet and Vagus Nerve

The vagus nerve utilizes synapses called acetylcholine as detachments to hand-off data along its superhighway. Along these lines, for instance, if there is irritation in the covering of the digestive organs, acetylcholine will tell the cerebrum. The mind will ideally enroll and report that this isn't a perfect long haul circumstance for the gut: supplements may not be ingested so well, and the gut covering may turn out to be harmed to such an extent that it can never again effectively keep poisons from entering the circulation system ("flawed gut"). The vagus nerve will at that point send more acetylcholine with relieving, calming directions from the mind back to the gut.1

Nourishments for Making Acetylcholine

Healthfully it might be astute to help crafted by the vagus nerve by giving nourishments that contain choline, so you can make more acetylcholine. Egg yolks are great wellsprings of choline in the event that they are delicate – or far better, crude, as you would discover, for instance, in new, custom-made mayonnaise. If you cook your egg yolks more, they will contain less choline. Offal is likewise a decent source, for example liver and kidneys. In either case, I would prescribe a natural field that encouraged hotspot for neatness and quality. For a vegetarian choice, lecithin granules (for the most part from soya, occasionally from sunflower seeds) are extraordinary to sprinkle onto nourishments and into smoothies.

You can likewise guarantee a sufficient admission of L-acetyl carnitine (in meat), nutrient B5 (in broccoli, chard, squash, sunflower seeds and eggs) and alpha-lipoic corrosive (from red meat, offal or brewers' yeast) to help with acetylcholine generation. Veggie lover and the individuals who eat low measures of meat can absorb L-acetyl carnitine from lysine and methionine: 2 amino acids typically present in the fish and spirulina.

An investigation done at The Feinstein Institute for Medical Research has indicated that the vagus nerve may really be what they call "the missing connection" to treating ceaseless aggravation that can cause an assortment of different issues - like hypertension, headaches, stomach related problems and any fiery related things like joint pain and so on. All without drugs!

Your Vagal Tone

Vagal tone basically alludes to the inhibitory control of your vagus nerve over your pulse. What the investigations presently show is that vagal tone is vital to initiating your parasympathetic sensory system and all that it does. We can quantify your vagal tone by following your pulse in blend with your breathing rate. Ordinarily, when you inhale, your pulse speeds somewhat and the other way around, and when you inhale out, your vagal tone is then controlled by the contrast between your inward breath pulse and your exhalation pulse. The greater the distinction, the higher your vagal tone, which is in reality great for this situation since it implies that you are more capable than somebody with a bring down vagal volume, to loosen up your body after an unpleasant circumstance.

Why a higher vagal tone is great

Aside from having the option to loosen up quicker after pressure, individuals with a high vagal tone have by and large better working interior frameworks including:

- Better glucose guideline
- Decreased danger of stroke and cardiovascular malady
- Generally lower circulatory strain
- Better absorption because of appropriate creation of stomach related proteins
- Fewer headaches

- Less despondency
- Less uneasiness (they normally manage pressure better)

What researchers have found out is that, the vagus nerve continually screens your gut's microbiome to decide whether there are any pathogenic living beings. And assuming this is the case, it starts a reaction that at that point controls any irritation that outcomes from these remote life forms, which can influence your state of mind, your feelings of anxiety (and your capacity to adapt to the pressure) and your general aggravation levels.

Healthy Daily Routines for Vagus Nerve

Regardless of the healthful ampleness of the suppers and tidbits, it is in like manner imperative to counsel with your essential consideration supplier or a Registered Dietitian to assist you with distinguishing nourishing needs altered to you.

Day 1

Breakfast:

- 1 serving of cereal (½ cup dry oats) arranged with one cup water or skim milk, 1 cut banana, 1 tablespoon of nut spread, and a scramble of cinnamon

Lunch:

- 1 meal meat move up: Spread mustard on an entire wheat wrap includes four cuts of dish hamburger, four meager cuts of tomatoes, ½ cup of lettuce, and ½ cup of red or green peppers. Firmly fold at that point cut into four equivalent areas.
- 1 medium banana

Supper:

- 1 serving of this Greek stuffed peppers formula
- 1 cup green beans sautéed in a ½ tablespoon of olive oil

Daily Tip:

Make oats medium-term for a speedy, healthy breakfast.

Day 2

Breakfast:

- 1 veggie omelet, likewise not hesitating to change veggies to preferring
- 1 cup of blueberries or grapes

Lunch:

- 1 serving of fish plate of mixed greens: Mix a 5-ounce jar of wild tuna fish with a little avocado, diced carrots and celery, a tablespoon of a lemon squeeze, and salt and pepper to taste. Devour as seems to be, top onto 2 cuts of entire grain bread, or plunge with cut ringer peppers, cucumbers cuts, or carrot sticks
- 1 medium apple

Supper:

- 1 side serving of mixed greens with 1 to cups of crude spinach leaves, tomatoes, and cucumber cuts bested with Greek yogurt farm dressing
- 1 serving eggplant pizza

Daily Tip:

Get the entire family required for a pizza party! Set out irregular fixings and enable them to dress their very own pizza.

Day 3

Breakfast:

- 1 yogurt-filled melon: Start by on a level plane cut the melon into equal parts. Spoon out the mash and seeds, scoop Greek yogurt into the made "bowl" inside the emptied melon, and sprinkle with

nuts or seeds for an additional crunch.

Lunch:

- 1 turkey sandwich: 2 cuts of entire grain bread, 4 ounces of cut turkey, arranged veggies, as blended greens and cut tomatoes. Smear the bread with 1 tablespoon mustard or olive oil-based mayo.
- ½ cup curds
- ½ cup pineapple pieces

Supper:

- 1 serving mango and avocado plate of mixed greens
- 2 fish tacos with broccoli slaw

Daily Tip:

Instead of obtaining bundled lunchmeat, get it directly from the butcher in the store to bring down sodium content. Bread is likewise a typical wellspring of sodium, so be watchful for low-sodium brands, or if nothing else providing 140 mg sodium or less per serving.

Day 4

Breakfast:

- 1 yogurt parfait: 1 cup plain Greek yogurt, 1 cup crisp blueberries, 1 tablespoon cleaved nuts, 1 tablespoon nectar, run of cinnamon

Lunch:

- 1 serving of cleaved chicken plate of mixed greens: Top three ounces of slashed chicken, two tablespoons of disintegrated low-fat bleu cheddar, ½ cup of hacked cucumbers, 1 tablespoon of hacked walnuts and dried cranberries on 2 cups of a cleaved serving of mixed greens hurled with 2 tablespoons of vinaigrette
- 1 orange

Supper:

- 4-ounces simmered turkey bosom
- ½ cup wild rice and mushroom pilaf
- 1 cup steamed broccoli

Daily Tip:

After supper, walk the family hound, bicycle around the area, or other physical movement to raise the pulse.

Day 5

Breakfast:

- 1 serving chocolate banana protein smoothie: Simply consolidate 1 scoop of chocolate protein powder (or enough for 25 to 30 grams of protein), 1 little banana (solidified), ½ cup milk of decision, 1 teaspoon dim chocolate, and ½ cup into a blender and blend until completely joined

Lunch:

- 1 hot refried dark spicy burro
- 1 cup cubed watermelon

Supper:

- ½ cup flame-broiled asparagus
- ¾ cup flame-broiled potatoes and peppers
- 1 jalapeno turkey burger

Daily Tip:

Add 1 to 2 tablespoons of chia or flax seeds to the smoothie for included heart-sound fiber and omega-3s.

Day 6

Breakfast:

- 1 serving high-protein flapjacks, beat with nutty spread, berries, and different top choices

Lunch:

- 1 serving smooth carrot and sweet potato soup
- 2 cups blended greens in with 1 cup of favored cleaved veggies (counting broccoli, carrot, and cucumber), 1 tablespoon balsamic vinegar

Supper:

- ½ cup heated coconut plantains
- ½ cup dark beans
- 1 serving pulled pork with salsa verde

Daily Tip:

Appreciate the scraps of the carrot and sweet potato soup by solidifying and warming when prepared to appreciate once more.

Day 7:

Breakfast:

- 1 avocado egg: Slice avocado into equal parts and take out the enormous pit. Split an egg into the made plunge and heat until the egg whites are cooked and the yolk is at an ideal solidness. Sprinkle on with green onions, diced tomatoes, and a bit of plain Greek yogurt. Shower with hot sauce for a little included zest!
- 1 navel orange

Lunch:

- 3-ounces flame-broiled chicken bosom
- 1 cup of quinoa tabbouleh

Supper:

- 1 serving Thai salmon bested onto ½ cup dark colored rice
- 1 cup steamed broccoli

Daily Tip:

Add flavor to the dark-colored rice with minced garlic and other most loved herbs and flavors. Likewise, cook your rice with different veggies for included fiber and micronutrients, alongside making it in enormous clumps for nutritious scraps to begin another week.

CONCLUSION

In conclusion, vagus nerve contributes to such a significant number of functions in our bodies, keeping it as "happy" as conceivably ought to be of prime significance. This doesn't imply that you need to stress over each easily overlooked detail you do. Just as with each side effect that appears as though identified with vagus nerve damage. Rather, watch and partake in those things that relax you and whatever makes you happy. Evade exorbitant drinking and propensities that lead to diabetes or related ailments. As you deal with your vagus nerve, it most likely deals with you consequently.

The Polyvagal Theory

The Complete Self-Help Guide to Manage Emotional Stress, Trauma, Phobias, Anxiety and Depression

© Copyright 2020 by LAYNE KELLY
All rights reserved

This document is geared towards providing exact and reliable information with regard to the topic and issue covered. The publication is sold with the idea that the publisher is not required to render accounting, officially permitted or otherwise qualified services. If advice is necessary, legal, or professional, a practiced individual in the profession should be ordered. From a Declaration of Principles which was accepted and approved equally by a Committee of the American Bar Association and a Committee of Publishers and Associations.

In no way is it legal to reproduce, duplicate, or transmit any part of this document in either electronic means or in printed format. Recording of this publication is strictly prohibited and any storage of this document is not allowed unless with written permission from the publisher. All rights reserved.

The information provided herein is stated to be truthful and consistent, in that any liability, in terms of inattention or otherwise, by any usage or abuse of any policies, processes, or directions contained within is the solitary and utter responsibility of the recipient reader. Under no circumstances will any legal responsibility or blame be held against the publisher for any reparation, damages, or monetary loss due to the information herein, either directly or indirectly.

Respective authors own all copyrights not held by the publisher.

The information herein is offered for informational purposes solely and is universal as so. The presentation of the information is without a contract or any type of guarantee assurance.

The trademarks that are used are without any consent, and the publication of the trademark is without permission or backing by the trademark owner. All trademarks and brands within this book are for clarifying purposes only and are owned by the owners themselves, not affiliated with this document

INTRODUCTION

The polyvagal theory portrays an autonomic sensory system that is impacted by the focal sensory system, touchy to afferent impacts, described by a versatile reactivity reliant on the phylogeny of the neural circuits, and intelligent with source cores in the brainstem managing the striated muscles of the face and head. The theory is reliant on collected information portraying the phylogenetic advances in the vertebrate autonomic sensory system. Its particular spotlight is on the phylogenetic move among reptiles and warm-blooded animals that brought about explicit changes to the vagal pathways directing the heart. As the source cores of the essential vagal efferent pathways managing the heart moved from the dorsal engine core of the vagus in reptiles to the core ambiguous in warm-blooded creatures, a face-heart association developed with rising properties of a social commitment framework that would empower social communications to control instinctive state.

Focal sensory system guideline of instinctive organs is the focal point of a few noteworthy distributions that have molded the surface of physiological request. For instance, in 1872, Darwin recognized the dynamic neural connection between the heart and the mind:

...at the point when the heart is influenced it responds on the mind; and the condition of the brain again responds through the pneumo-gastric [vagus] nerve on the heart; so that under any fervor there will be a lot of common activity and response between these, the two most significant organs of the body.

In spite of the fact that Darwin recognized the bidirectional correspondence between the viscera and the brain, resulting in a formal portrayal of the autonomic sensory system limited the significance of focal administrative structures and afferents. Following Langley, clinical and physiological research would, in general, spotlight on the fringe engine nerves of the autonomic anxious system, with a theoretical accentuation on the matched threat among thoughtful and parasympathetic efferent pathways on the objective instinctive organs. This center limited enthusiasm for both afferent pathways and the brainstem regions that manage explicit efferent pathways.

The early conceptualization of the vagus concentrated on an undifferentiated efferent pathway that was accepted to balance "tone" simultaneously to a few objective organs. In this way, brainstem zones controlling the supradiaphragmatic (e.g., myelinated vagal pathways beginning in the core ambiguous and ending fundamentally over the stomach) were not practically recognized from those directing the subdiaphragmatic (e.g., unmyelinated vagal pathways starting in the dorsal engine core of the vagus and ending principally underneath the stomach). Without this differentiation, research and theory concentrated on the combined hostility between the parasympathetic and thoughtful innervation to the target organs. The outcome of accentuation on matched opposition was an acknowledgment in physiology and medication of worldwide builds, for example, autonomic equalization, thoughtful tone, and vagal tone.

Over 50 years back, Hess recommended that the autonomic sensory system was not exclusively vegetative and programmed but rather was rather a coordinated framework with both fringe and focal neurons. By underlining the focal components that intervene in the dynamic guideline of fringe organs, Hess foresaw the requirement for advances to ceaselessly screen fringe and focal neural circuits engaged with the guideline of instinctive capacity.

CHAPTER ONE:
POLYVAGAL THEORY IN PRACTICE

Picturing brain chemistry can be something like envisioning a tropical storm. Although we can envision a terrible climate, it is hard to envision changing that climate. However, Stephen Porges' polyvagal theory gives advocates a valuable image of the sensory system that can direct us in our endeavors to support customers.

Porges' polyvagal theory created out of his examinations with the vagus nerve. The vagus nerve serves the parasympathetic sensory system, which is the quieting part of our sensory system mechanics. The parasympathetic piece of the autonomic sensory system adjusts the thoughtful dynamic part, yet is considerably more nuanced ways than we comprehended before polyvagal theory.

Our three-section sensory system

Before polyvagal theory, our sensory system was imagined as a two-section opposing framework, with more initiation flagging not so much quieting but rather more quieting flagging less enactment. The polyvagal theory distinguishes the third sort of sensory system reaction that is called the social commitment framework, a lively blend of actuation and quieting that works out of one of a kind nerve impact.

The social commitment framework encourages us to explore connections. Helping our customers move into the utilization of their social commitment framework permits them to turn out to be progressively adaptable in their adapting styles.

The two different pieces of our sensory system capacity to assist us with overseeing dangerous circumstances, most advisors are now acquainted with the two guard instruments activated by these two pieces of the sensory system: thoughtful battle or-flight and parasympathetic shutdown, now and again called freeze-or-black out. Utilization of our social commitment framework, then again, requires a feeling of wellbeing.

Polyvagal theory causes us to comprehend that the two parts of the vagus nerve quiet the body, yet they do as such in various manners. Shutdown, or freeze-or-black out, happens through the dorsal part of the vagus nerve. This response can feel like the exhausted muscles and discombobulation of an awful influenza. At the point when the dorsal vagal nerve closes down the body, it can move us into stability or separation. Notwithstanding influencing the heart and lungs, the dorsal branch influences the body working underneath the stomach and is associated with stomach related problems. The central part of the vagal nerve influences the body working over the stomach. This is the branch that serves the social commitment framework. The ventral vagal nerve hoses the body's consistently dynamic state. Picture controlling a pony as you ride it back to the stable. You would keep on pulling back on and discharge the reins in nuanced approaches to guarantee that the pony keeps up a proper speed. In like manner, the ventral vagal nerve permits initiation in a nuanced way, in this way offering an unexpected quality in comparison to thoughtful enactment.

Ventral vagal discharge into movement takes milliseconds, while thoughtful actuation takes seconds and includes different synthetic responses that are much the same as losing the pony's reins. What's more, when the battle or-flight compound responses have started, it can take our bodies 10–20 minutes to come back to our pre-battle/pre-flight state. Ventral vagal discharge into movement doesn't include these sorts of synthetic responses. Subsequently, we can make snappier alterations among initiation and quieting, like what we can do when we utilize the reins to control the pony.

In the event that you go to a canine park, you will see certain pooches that are apprehensive. They display battle or-flight practices. Different mutts will flag a desire to play. This flagging frequently takes the structure that we people seized for the descending confronting hound present in yoga. At the point when a canine gives this sign, it signals a degree of excitement that can be extraordinary. Be that as it may, this perky vitality has an altogether different soul than the force of battle or-flight practices. This energetic soul portrays the social commitment framework. At the point when we experience our condition as protected, we work from our social commitment framework.

Injury's impact on sensory system reaction

On the off chance that we have uncertain injury from quite a while ago, we may live in the form of ceaseless battle or-flight. We might have the option to channel this battle or-flight uneasiness into exercises, for example, cleaning the house, raking the forgets about or working at the rec center, yet these exercises will have an unexpected vibe in comparison to they would on the off chance that they were finished with social commitment science (think "Whistle While You Work").

For some injury survivors, no movement effectively channels their battle or-flight sensations. Therefore, they feel caught and their bodies shut down. These customers may live in a rendition of a never-ending shutdown.

Levine has considered the shutdown reaction through creature perceptions and bodywork with customers. He clarifies that rising up out of shutdown requires a shiver or shake to release suspended battle or-flight vitality. In a perilous circumstance, on the off chance that we have shut down and an open door for dynamic endurance introduces itself, we can wake ourselves up. As advisors, we may perceive this move from shutdown to battle or-trip in a customer's move from wretchedness into tension.

However, how might we help our customers move into their social commitment science? In the event that customers live in an increasingly dissociative, discouraged, shutdown way, we should assist them with moving briefly into battle or-flight. As customers experience battle or-flight power, we should then assist them with finding a feeling of security. At the point when they can detect that they are protected, they can move into their social commitment framework.

The body-mindfulness procedures that are a piece of cognitive conduct treatment (CBT) and dialectical conduct treatment (DBT) can assist customers with moving out of dissociative, shutdown reactions by urging them to turn out to be progressively typified. At the point when customers are increasingly present in their bodies and better ready to take care of transient solid strain, they can wake up from a shutdown reaction. As customers actuate out of shutdown and move toward battle or-flight sensations, the idea rebuilding methods that are additionally part of CBT and DBT can instruct customers to assess their security all the more precisely. Intelligent listening systems can assist customers with feeling an association with their advocates. This causes it feasible for these customers to feel sufficiently safe to move into social commitment science.

Explicit parts of ventral vagal nerve working

Porges picked the name social commitment framework on the grounds that the ventral vagal nerve influences the center ear, which sift through foundation clamors to make it simpler to hear the human voice. It additionally influences facial muscles and therefore the capacity to make informative outward appearances. At long last, it influences the larynx and hence vocal tone and vocal designing, helping people make sounds that calm each other.

Customers with poor social commitment framework working may have inward ear challenges that make it difficult for them to get relieving from others' voices. As guides, we can be aware of our vocal examples and outward appearances and inquisitive about the impacts those parts of our correspondence have on our customers.

In view of his comprehension of the impacts of the vagus nerve, Porges takes note of that broadening breathes out longer than breathes in for a while actuates the parasympathetic sensory system. Porges that was a clarinet player in his childhood recalls the impact of the breath designs required to play that instrument.

As a moving advisor, I am mindful that expanding breathes out helps customers who are stuck in types of battle or-flight reaction to move into a feeling of wellbeing. For customers stuck in some type of shutdown, I have discovered that cognizant breath-work can mix the battle or flight reaction. At the point when this happens, the battle or-flight vitality should be released through development for customers to discover a feeling of wellbeing. For example, these customers may need to run set up or punch a cushion. The chain of command of resistance framework working clarifies these remedial procedures.

Respiratory sinus arrhythmia is a decent file of ventral vagal working. This implies we presently have strategies to examine the viability of body treatments and expressive expressions treatments.

Polyvagal theory

What follows is a case of how I utilized polyvagal theory with a customer who experienced a clinical injury during her introduction to the world.

The customer, whom I have seen for quite a while, portrayed inclination drowsy and recognized experiencing issues finding a workable pace on this day. Her therapist had recommended her a medicine as a method for treating uneasiness mixed by the introduction of her girl's first youngster. The customer and I had recently standardized her uneasiness as an injury reaction.

During the prior year's coming to see me, this customer had endeavored suicide, which brought about clinical techniques that add to her injury. Through our work, she has come to comprehend that the fits of anxiety she has when in contained circumstances are additionally injury reactions. She has lived quite a bit of her life in interminable battle or-flight reaction mode.

On this day, she was alleviated to be less enthusiastic, yet she dreaded the tiredness that went with medicine's assistance in quieting her battle or-flight sensations. I considered this to be of the tiredness as a dread of a dorsal vagal shutdown. We examined the likelihood that this tiredness could permit her another sort of initiation. I inquired as to whether she might want to do some expressive craftsmanship that would permit delicate, expressive development. She shivered, naming her inclination for things that were less abstract.

We discussed the presence of a sort of aliveness that, despite everything, has a sense of security. We discussed the chance of existing in an energetic spot where there is no good and bad, just inclination. We recognized that since her introduction to the world, she and her folks had expected that her wellbeing would flop once more. This condition, wherein she had grown up, had bolstered sensory system working intended forever undermining circumstances. With medicines quieting her battle or-flight initiation, I recommended that maybe she could investigate some quieter, increasingly fun-loving sorts of emotional encounters.

"It feels like you are attempting to make an alternate me," she reacted. I recognized that it might seem as though I were suspecting she could be somebody she wasn't. Yet, I clarified that what I was really proposing was simply the likelihood that she could be in an alternate manner.

The customer revealed to me she had another book on grand-parenting that contained a part in the play. She said she would think about understanding it. Simultaneously, she said that she probably wouldn't have the option to endure the medicine and might need to get off of it. In any case, the possibility of this unique, increasingly lively method for being has been acquainted with her and, for a minute or two, experienced.

Getting the picture

As instructors equipped with a polyvagal theory, we can picture resistance component chain of command. We can perceive shifts from battle or-trip to close down when customers feel caught. We can likewise perceive the development from shutdown into battle or-flight that offers a potential move into social commitment science if and when the customer can increase a feeling of wellbeing.

Before the polyvagal theory, most instructors could likely perceive battle or-flight and shutdown practices. They could presumably detect contrast between barrier reactions intended forever, compromising circumstances and reactions that are called the social commitment framework. The polyvagal theory extends that mindfulness with the information that fun-loving excitement and therapeutic give up have an interesting sensory system impact.

Most advocates acknowledge brain chemistry; however, they may think that it's hard to picture how to utilize the data. On account of the polyvagal theory's explanation of the job of the central part of the vagus nerve, we presently have a guide to direct us.

CHAPTER TWO:
POLYVAGAL THEORY AND HOW IT RELATES TO SOCIAL CUES

Have you at any point been in a circumstance where you feel unsure or in harm's way however not so much sure why? You may glance around and see that nobody else is by all accounts irritated, yet something despite everything feels off to you?

You may not understand it; however, you are strolling around on the planet every day, perusing a great many meaningful gestures in your condition. In our collaboration with others, we get outward appearances, manners of speaking, substantial development, and the sky is the limit from there. We are continually bustling watching and communicating with the world and others as a feature of the human experience.

As we have these communications with others, our feeling of self is being molded. We find out about ourselves and about others, who we can trust, and who feels hazardous to us. Our bodies are preparing this kind of data continually through these associations with the world.

The Body's Surveillance System

Our sensory system is an unpredictable structure that accumulates data from all over our body and facilitates movement. There are two fundamental pieces of the sensory system: the focal sensory system and the fringe sensory system.

Focal Sensory System

The focal sensory system comprises of two structures:
- Brain. This is the structure made out of billions of interconnected neurons or nerve cells contained in the skull and capacities as the

planning place for practically the entirety of our body's capacities. It is the seat of our acumen.
- Spinal line. This is a packaged system of nerve filaments, interfacing most pieces of our body to our brain.

Fringe Sensory System

The fringe sensory system comprises the entirety of the nerves outside of our mind and spinal line. It tends to be ordered into two particular frameworks:

- Somatic sensory system (willful). This framework permits our muscles and brains to speak with one another. The physical framework enables our mind and spinal rope to impart signs to our muscles to assist them with moving, just as sends data from the body back to the brain and spinal rope.
- Autonomic sensory system (automatic). This is the framework that controls the organs and interior organs, for example, the heart, lungs, and stomach related framework. These are, basically, the things that run our body without us having to purposefully consider them. For instance, we can inhale without contemplating taking a breath each time.

Perusing Danger Cues

Our autonomic sensory system (the automatic framework that assists with controlling things like our breathing, pulse, assimilation, and salivation) is unpredictable and constantly occupied. Notwithstanding running these significant capacities in our bodies, for example, helping us inhale, helping our heart siphon, and helping us digest nourishment, our autonomic sensory system is likewise helping us to check, decipher, and react to risk prompts.

There are two separate frameworks grinding away inside the autonomic sensory system that is helping us to peruse and react to risk signals:

- Sympathetic sensory system. This framework is associated with stimulating our bodies to react by activating us to move when in risky circumstances. Many allude to this framework as provoking our "battle or flight" responses to threat signs in our condition. It is likewise liable for enacting our adrenal organs to discharge epinephrine into our circulation system, also called an adrenaline surge. At the point when we see a snake, our thoughtful sensory system will peruse the sign of the potential risk and brief our body to react, likely including a fast adrenaline surge and us promptly moving endlessly from the snake.

- Parasympathetic sensory system. This framework is associated with quieting our bodies, saving vitality as it does things like moderate our pulse, manage our assimilation and lower our circulatory strain. Some allude to this framework as the "rest and summary" framework. As we read that a prompt isn't risky, our body starts to quiet with the assistance of our parasympathetic sensory system.

The Vagus Nerve

There is one nerve, specifically, that is important to The Polyvagal Theory: The vagus nerve.

The vagus nerve is the tenth cranial nerve, a long and meandering nerve that starts at the medulla oblongata. This piece of the brain, the medulla oblongata, is situated in the lower some portion of the mind, sitting simply above where the brain interfaces with our spinal rope.

There are different sides to this vagus nerve, the dorsal (back) and the ventral (front). From that point, the different sides of the vagus nerve run down all through our body, considered to have the most extensive dispersion of the considerable number of nerves inside the human body.

Filtering our Environment

From the time we are conceived, we are instinctively checking our condition for prompts of security and threat.

A child reacts to the sheltered sentiments of closeness with their parent or guardian. In like manner, an infant will react to signals that are seen as unnerving or risky, similar to a more odd, an alarming clamor, or an absence of reaction from their guardian. We filter for signs of wellbeing and peril our whole lives.

Perception

The polyvagal theory depicts the procedure where our neural circuits are perusing prompts of threat in our condition as neuroception. Through this procedure of neuroception, we are encountering the world in a manner by which we are automatically examining circumstances and individuals to decide whether they are sheltered or perilous.

As a component of our autonomic sensory system, this procedure is going on without us in any event, staying alert that it is going on. Similarly, as we can inhale without having to purposefully instruct ourselves to calmly inhale; we can check our condition for prompts without guiding ourselves to do as such. The vagus nerve is specifically noteworthy during this procedure of neuroception.

During the time spent neuroception, the two sides of our vagus nerve can be invigorated. Each side (ventral and dorsal) has been found to react in particular manners as we sweep and procedure data from our condition and social co-operations.

The ventral (front) side of the vagus nerve reacts to prompts of wellbeing in our condition and collaborations. It bolsters sentiments of physical security and being securely sincerely associated with others in our social condition.

The dorsal (posterior of the vagus nerve reacts to signals of peril, it pulls us away from the association, out of mindfulness, and into a condition of self-assurance. In minutes when we may encounter a sign of extraordinary risk, we can close down and feel solidified, a sign that our dorsal vagal nerve has dominated.

Three Developmental Stages of Response

The polyvagal theory portrays three transformative stages engaged with the advancement of our autonomic sensory system. Instead of just proposing that there is a harmony between our thoughtful and parasympathetic sensory system, The theory describe that there is really a chain of command of reactions incorporated with our autonomic sensory system.

- Immobilization. Portrayed as the most seasoned pathway, this includes an immobilization reaction. As you would recollect the dorsal (posterior of the vagus nerve react to signs of extraordinary risk, this implies we would react to our dread by getting solidified, numb, and closing down. As though our parasympathetic sensory system is kicking into overdrive, our reaction really brings about us freezing, as opposed to just backing off.
- Mobilization. Inside this reaction, we are taken advantage of our thoughtful sensory system which, as you may recall, is the framework that causes us to activate notwithstanding a risk signal. We get a move on our adrenaline race to escape from peril or to fend off our risk. The polyvagal theory proposes that this pathway was besides creating in the transformative pecking order.
- Social commitment. The most current expansion to the progression of reactions, this is situated in our ventral (front) side of the vagus nerve. Recollecting that this piece of the vagus nerve reacts to sentiments of wellbeing and association, social commitment permits us to feel secured and is encouraged by that ventral vagus pathway. Right now, you can have a sense of security, quiet, associated, and locked in.

The Response Hierarchy in Daily Life

As we experience life connecting with the world, there are unavoidably those minutes when we will have a sense of security and others or in which we will feel inconvenience or threat. The polyvagal theory proposes that this space is liquid for us and we can move all through these better places inside the progressive system of reactions.

We may encounter social commitment in the grasp of a safe cherished one and, around the same time, wind up in preparation as we are stood up to with threat, for example, an out of control hound, a theft, or an extraordinary clash with an associate.

There are times when we may peruse and react to a risk sign and procedure the circumstance such that drives us to feel caught and incapable of escaping the circumstance. In those minutes, our body is reacting to expanded sentiments of threat and trouble, moving into an increasingly basic space of immobilization. Our dorsal vagus nerve is being affected and securing us to a position of freezing, feeling numb and, as certain scientists accept, separation.

The risk signs can turn out to be excessively overpowering in those minutes and we see no reasonable way out. A case of this could be snapshots of sexual or physical maltreatment.

Effect of Trauma

At the point when somebody has encountered an injury, especially in encounters where they were left immobilized, their capacity to examine their condition for peril prompts can get slanted. Obviously, our body will probably help us never experience an unnerving minute like that again, so it will do whatever it needs to do so as to help secure us.

Our social commitment permits us to associate all the more smoothly with others, feeling associated and safe. At the point when our body gets a prompt inside a collaboration that signals we may not be sheltered, it starts to react. For some, this sign may move them into a position of an activation reaction, getting a move on the endeavor to kill the risk or escape from the danger.

For the individuals who have encountered an injury, the sign of a threat prompt can move them straightforwardly from social commitment to immobilization. Astonishingly partner various relational prompts as risky, for example, a slight difference in outward appearance, a specific manner of speaking, or particular sorts of body posing, they can wind up returning to a position of reaction that is recognizable to them with an end goal to get ready and secure themselves.

A reaction of assembly may not be enrolled by the body as an alternative. This can be very confounding for injury survivors, ignorant of how this pecking order of a reaction is affected by their communications with others and the world.

Association and Polyvagal Theory

In spite of the fact that the vagus nerve is known for being generally circulated and associated with an assortment of regions of the body, note that this framework can impact cranial nerves that control social commitment through outward appearance and vocalization. As people who are wired for association, we can see how filtering for peril prompts can happen every now and again in our communications with our loved one or significant strong others in our lives.

We naturally long for sentiments of wellbeing, trust, and solace in our associations with others and rapidly get prompts that reveal to us when we may not be sheltered. As individuals become more secure with and for one another, it very well may be simpler to manufacture sound bonds, share vulnerabilities, and experience closeness with one another.

CHAPTER THREE: POLYVAGAL THEORY SIMPLIFIED

The polyvagal theory clarifies three distinct pieces of our sensory system and their reactions to distressing circumstances. When we comprehend those three sections, we can perceive any reason why and how we respond to high measures of pressure.

On the off chance that polyvagal theory sounds as energizing as watching paint dry, stay, trust me. It's an entrancing clarification of how our body handles enthusiastic pressure, and how we can utilize various treatments to revise the impact of injury.

For what reason is the polyvagal theory significant?

For specialists and pop-brain research aficionado the same, understanding polyvagal theory can help with:

- Understanding injury and PTSD
- Understanding the move of assault and withdrawal seeing someone
- Understanding how extraordinary pressure prompts separation or closing down
- Understanding how to peruse non-verbal communication

We like to think about our feelings as ethereal, complex, and hard to arrange and distinguish.

In all actuality, feelings are reactions to an improvement (inner or outer). Regularly they occur out of our mindfulness, particularly in the event that we are withdrawn or incongruent, with our internal enthusiastic life.

Our base wants to remain alive. This is essential to our body. That is the place the polyvagal theory comes in to play.

The sensory system is continually running out of sight, controlling our body capacities so we can consider different things—like what sort of dessert we'd prefer to request, or how to get that An in medications school. The whole sensory system works a couple with the brain and can assume control over our enthusiastic experience, regardless of whether we don't need it to.

An anecdote about a gazelle...

Creatures are an incredible case of how we handle pressure, since they respond basely, without mindfulness. They do what we would, on the off chance that we weren't so very much restrained.

On the off chance that you have ever viewed a National Geographic Africa extraordinary, you've seen a lioness pursue a gazelle. A gathering of gazelles is brushing, and out of nowhere, one gazes upward, hyper mindful of what's going on around him, the entire gathering notification and focuses.

After a minute, the lioness begins her pursuit. The gazelle she's singled out runs as quickly as possible (thoughtful sensory system) until he is gotten. At the point when he is gotten, he immediately goes limp (parasympathetic sensory system).

The lioness hauls the gazelle back to her offspring, where they start to play with it before they go in for the murder. In the event that the lioness gets occupied, and the gazelle sees a snapshot of chance, he's up and dashing off once more, seeming as though he unexpectedly returned to life (once more into thoughtful sensory system reaction).

At the point when the gazelle was gotten, with teeth around his neck, his shutdown reaction kicked in - he solidified. Whenever he saw the chance to run, his battle or flight kicked in, and he ran.

The polyvagal theory covers those three states—association, battle or flight, or shutdown.

Here's the way they work...

Association Mode

Or...rest and relaxation...or myelinated vagus nerve of the parasympathetic sensory system originating from the core uncertain reaction

During non-unpleasant circumstances, on the off chance that we are sincerely sound, our bodies remain in a social commitment state, or a cheerful, typical, non-go crazy state.

I like to call it "association." By association, I imply that we are fit for "associated" cooperation with another person. We are strolling near, unafraid, making the most of our day, eating with loved ones and our body and feelings feel typical.

It's likewise called ventral vagal reaction since that is the piece of the mind that is initiated during association mode. It resembles a green light for ordinary life.

What does this look like and feel?

- Our resistant framework is sound.
- We feel typical bliss, transparency, harmony, and interest in existence.
- We are resting soundly and eating typically.
- Our face is expressive.
- We sincerely identify with others.
- We all the more effectively comprehend and tune in to other people.
- Our body feels quiet and grounded.

Freeze, Flight, Fight, or Puff Up

...or on the other hand the thoughtful sensory system reaction

The thoughtful sensory system is our prompt response to push that influences almost every organ in the body.

The thoughtful sensory system causes that "battle or flight" state we have all known about. It gives us those prompts with the goal that it can keep us alive.

How does this occur? What does this look like and feel?

- We sense the risk and stick to check the environmental factors for genuine peril.
- We discharge cortisol, epinephrine and norepinephrine to enable us to achieve what we have to - escape or battle our foe.
- Our heartbeat spikes, we sweat, and we feel more prepared.
- We feel restless, apprehensive, or irate.
- There might be flashes of outward appearances of dread and outrage, with the foundation of all the more a despite everything face. In the event that positive feelings are available, they generally look constrained.
- Our absorption eases back down as blood races to the muscles.
- Our veins tighten to the digestion tracts and expand to the muscles expected to run or battle.
- We might need to flee, or punch somebody, or respond genuinely here and there, or simply puff-up and look frightening.
- Our muscles may feel tense, electric, tight, vibrating, throbbing, trembling, and hard.
- Our hands might be moist.
- Our stomach might be agonizingly tied.
- All our faculties' center.
- Our motions may show guarding of our crucial organs, clench hands gripped or puffing ourselves up to look greater or more grounded.

In battle or flight, at some level, we accept we can at present endure whatever risk we believe is hazardous.

Close Down

...or then again the Unmyelinated Vagus of the Parasympathetic Sensory System originating from the Dorsal Motor Nucleus

What's intriguing about this piece of the parasympathetic sensory system? Its capacity is to keep us solidified as a versatile instrument to assist us with getting by to either battle or flight once more.

At the point when David Livingston was assaulted by a lion, he later revealed, "it caused a kind of vagueness in which there was no feeling of torment nor sentiment of fear, however very aware of every one of that was going on."

At the point when our thoughtful sensory system has kicked into overdrive, we despite everything can't get away and feel looming passing the dorsal vagal parasympathetic sensory system takes control.

It causes freezing or shutdown, as a type of self-safeguarding. (Consider somebody who drops under outrageous pressure.)

What does this look like and feel?

- Emotionally, it feels like separation, deadness, bleary-eyed, misery, disgrace, a feeling of feeling caught, out of the body, disengaged from the world
- Our eyes may watch fixed and scattered
- The dorsal engine core through the unmyelinated vagus nerve diminishes our pulse, circulatory strain, outward appearances, sexual and resistant reaction frameworks
- We might be activated to feel sickened, hurl, crap, precipitously pee
- We may feel low or no torment
- Our lungs (bronchi) contract and we inhale slower
- We may experience issues getting words out or feel choking around our throat
- Our brain has diminished digestion and this causes lost body

mindfulness, limp appendages, diminished capacity to think plainly, and diminished capacity to set down account recollections
- Our body stance may fall or twist up in a ball

In shutdown mode, at some level, our sensory system accepts we are in a hazardous circumstance, and it attempts to keep us alive through keeping our body still.

A few people who have had both connection injury and consequent injury can have ceaseless suicidality and separation scenes that last days to months. Research shows that long haul arrangements include:

- Dialectical conduct treatment
- Mentalization-based treatment
- Transference centered treatment

How injury influences the sensory system

As people, we do a similar thing as that gazelle when we see enthusiastic or physical risk. We switch back and forth between quiet touching (parasympathetic - association mode), battle or flight (thoughtful framework battle and flight) or shutdown (parasympathetic-shut down mode).

Our reaction is all in our view of the occasion. Possibly somebody was simply playing a game when they leaped out to unnerve us, yet we swooned. Whatever the explanation, regardless of whether the episode was purposeful or not, our body moved into shutdown mode, we enrolled it as an injury. Our body moved into shutdown mode.

Or on the other hand, perhaps the injury occasion was true, hazardous, and our sensory system reacted suitably to the boosts.

Regardless of what the reason was, our mind accepted what was going on was dangerous enough that it made our body go into battle, flight, or shutdown mode.

On the off chance that somebody has experienced such a horrendous mishap, that their body tips into shutdown reaction, any occasion that helps the individual to remember that dangerous event can trigger them into disengagement or separation once more.

Individuals can even live in a condition of separation or shut down for a considerable length of time or month's one after another.

Veterans regularly experience this during boisterous, abrupt commotions, for example, firecrackers or tempests. A lady who was assaulted may rapidly switch into the hypervigilant or separated reaction in the event that she feels somebody is following her. Somebody who was manhandled may be activated when much someone else begins shouting.

The issue happens when we haven't prepared the first injury so that the first injury is settled.

That is the thing that PTSD (post-awful pressure issue) is—our body's eruption to a little reaction, and either stuck in battle and flight or shut down.

Individuals who experience injury and the shutdown reaction typically feel disgrace around their failure to act, when their body didn't move. They regularly wish they would have battled more during those minutes.

A Vietnam vet may feel they bombed their partners who passed on around them while they stood, solidified in dread. An unfortunate assault casualty may feel the individual in question didn't fend off their attacker since they solidified. A casualty of misuse may feel they quit attempting to get away from their abuser, and that they are frail or fizzled.

Quite a bit of "stress" preparing, which trains individuals to keep on staying in battle and flight mode, intends to keep individuals out of separation during the reality of passing circumstances. Sadly, these practices aren't regular past world-class sports groups or unique powers. The perfect measure of worry, with great recuperation, can lead our sensory systems into more significant levels of adjustment.

Leaving shutdown mode

So how would we move to pull out of shutdown mode?

Something contrary to the dorsal vagal framework is the social commitment framework.

In this way, to put it plainly, what fixes shutdown mode is bringing somebody into sound social commitment, or legitimate connection.

Getting down into the stray pieces of how this functions in our body can assist us with understanding why we feel the manner in which we do truly when your body is in battle, flight, or shut down mode.

At the point when we comprehend why our body responds to the manner in which it does, similar to a series of signs and some fundamental science about the brain, we can see how to switch states. We can start to move out of the battle or flight state, out of the shutdown mode, and go into the social commitment state.

As specialists, regardless of whether we are simply setting up an association with another, on edge patients, or helping them manage their most profound horrendous recollections, realizing how to explore the polyvagal states is significant.

It can likewise be useful in the event that you have recently distinguished yourself in a portion of these side effects. For example, "When I'm with my folks, even as an Adult and they begin battling, I feel dizzy and disengaged."

In the event that you've seen a portion of these things in yourself, ideally through treatment, and in any event, seeing how this works, you can haul yourself out of a disengaged state.

Studies show that a few pieces of the mind shut down during the review of awful accidents, including the verbal focuses and the thinking places of the brain.

This is the reason it's essential to direct treatment, or leaving shutdown mode, in a sheltered, sound way, in a protected, solid condition. This is the reason a positive connection is basic. Else, you risk re-traumatizing the patient.

Since I am a specialist, I will compose this to exhibit how to enable a patient change to out of shutdown mode.

Nonetheless, these tips despite everything apply to the individuals who are simply seeing how shutdown mode functions. Furthermore, it can even assist the individuals who feel shut down to start to realize how to attempt to achieve a sound social commitment mode once more.

- Have a trust-based relationship. Due to the possibility to re-damage, don't address seriously awful mishaps—particularly ones where you think shutdown mode kicked in until the helpful relationship feels profoundly associated.

It's significant as the specialist to permit the patient to communicate things they couldn't communicate to others—despicable sentiments, outrage, sexual reaction, anything that feels startling to impart to other people.

- Find your own quiet place. On the off chance that you can identify with their misery, remain at the time with them, and assist them with feeling associated during their shutdown, you are tossing them a lifesaver. You're helping them leave shutdown, into social commitment.

It's critical to the battle against the inclination to separate, regardless of how abhorrent the topic is. As advisors, we could separate due to the mirror neuron reaction - to reflect our patient's mind, and in light of the fact that when hearing horrendous injury, it's anything but difficult to envision it transpiring.

The human experience is amazing to such an extent that when we reconnect the injury, with another person to help us, it revamps that occasion in our brain, including the sentiment of being bolstered inside the injury memory. We make new neural pathways around the injury, and we can change our body's reaction to it.

- Let the patient lead. Try not to go on a witch chase. On the off chance that the patient brings it up, incline toward the subject. Be that as it may, it is destructive to incite the patient into something

- that isn't there by posing driving inquiries and attempting to get them to admit. Try not to let your own experience lead you to envision they have additionally experienced something.
- Normalize their reaction. The whole polyvagal theory should make our state "thank you!" to our bodies, regardless of whether that framework is overactive now and again - baseless frenzy - that our body is looking out for us, attempting to keep us alive.

Our body responding in that manner is a similar thing as the gazelle either fleeing or going limp. What's more, gazelles have no clue what feelings are in any case.

Since the patient comprehends that their passionate reaction was versatile, base, and fitting, we can dispose of the disgrace that their non-response caused.

- Help them discover their annoyance. Outrage is an extraordinarily versatile feeling, and it's one we don't permit ourselves to have. We think the outrage is terrible. However, outrage gives us where our sound limits were crossed.

Outrage gives us vitality to conquer the deterrent. We can help the patient see they had the enthusiastic vitality to survive, yet the vitality couldn't be shown at the time they needed it.

On the off chance that, in a meeting, we can get a patient to distinguish their annoyance, they will see that they were not totally inert to the awful accident. On the off chance that we can enable them to feel even the littlest development of a micro-expression of outrage all over - the slight downturn of the internal eyebrows - we can show them their body didn't thoroughly sell out them at that time.

We can reconnect their body and their sentiments to their feelings. This builds up a condition of consistency - where their inside sentiments coordinate their external exhibitions of those emotions.

Further, as a dissociative memory is investigated, discovering outrage and decreasing disgrace takes into account the memory to in a general sense change. Outrage brings them out of separation, regardless of whether it is outrage at you, the specialist!

- Introduce body development. Since shutdown makes us freeze, reactivating body developments while discussing the injury is an extraordinary method to reconnect the body and psyche, to bring them out of shutdown.

For instance, one of my patients was in a mishap. At the point when the EMS appeared, they lashed her to a gurney to stack her into the rear of a rescue vehicle. More than the genuine mishap, being caught on that gurney was horrendous for her. For the whole ride to the emergency clinic, she was startled that she'd hurt her neck, and the entirety of the tension that encompasses a neck injury made her be solidified in dread. Indeed, even in discussing the injury in the treatment meeting, her body was firm, solidified, and she was separating.

I asked her, "How might you have needed to move during that minute?" She said she would have needed her arms to have the option to move. I asked her to gradually, carefully, move her arms in the manner in which she would have needed to.

It's critical to do the development carefully and gradually, concentrating on the vibe of the development. That patient felt an enormous arrival of vitality. In the accompanying meetings, she had the option to tell the memory as an account, rather than separating.

Having the patient move - slow punching, kicking, contorting, running set up - flips the individual from shutdown into the battle or flight mode, with the objective being to move into association, or social commitment, mode.

Body development works out, related to conversing with an advisor, can essentially change the memory.

- Practicing confidence. Enthusiastic shutdown can happen inside connections where one individual feels they can't speak with the other individual well.

One specialist, John Gottman, depicts this training as stonewalling. Rehearsing self-assuredness can help the patient feel more in charge of their passionate state, and have a sense of security to move into sound relationship designs.

- Breath-work, care, and yoga all have a job in getting increasingly associated with your present time and place body. I will examine this subject finally in a future digital broadcast.

Showing yourself how to all the more likely ensure yourself, later on, can be ground-breaking and furthermore resets the pressure framework after some time. I discussed quality preparing in an earlier scene, and later on, will discuss figuring out how to battle as a functioning method to not stay detached or an unfortunate casualty both in outlook and capacity. Further accomplishing something hard, on a progressing premise, considers building inward quality which can keep you in battle and flight longer before going into shut down.

CHAPTER FOUR: CHILDREN, EMOTIONAL REGULATION, AND POLYVAGAL THEORY

As Parents, our duty is to assist kids with handling through their encounters. This isn't a simple assignment. It is anything but difficult to feel activated by kids' huge feelings, regardless of whether it is dread, outrage, or pity; particularly when the declaration of these sentiments turns out as troublesome practices. The polyvagal theory enables Parents to explore your youngster's extremely enthusiastic states.

Kids may get resistant, decline to rest, begin lying, or become forceful with kin or Parents. As parents, it isn't unexpected to endeavor to apply outcomes or rebuff our youngsters. In any case, this can decline into a battle of will, where Parents would prefer not to be the first to yield. While limit setting is important to guard our kids and ourselves, it is basic that we help our kids loosen up their passionate dysregulation in the security of a mindful relationship.

Polyvagal Theory gives a neurobiological system to understanding the association between the brain, body, and feelings. Enabled with more profound comprehension, we increment our ability to sympathetically and effectively bolster youngsters' passionate guidelines.

Being a sentiments analyst

Youngsters need Adults to assist them with handling through their passionate reactions to the world; sentiments that happen during ordinary formative achievements and furthermore from upsetting or awful life occasions. There are times in parenting where you have to play the job of investigator to decide the reason for your kid's misery. Is it hunger, insufficient rest, tactile based, an adjustment in the schedule, kin elements, or an occasion that occurred at school?

As Parents, when we associate with youngsters who are dysregulated inwardly, we frequently feel upset as well. On the off chance that you see your kid feeling on edge almost certainly, you will feel stressed for your youngster and may even scrutinize your parenting aptitudes. On the off chance that a youngster is attempting to hit you, it is entirely expected to feel irate, frightful, or guarded. On the off chance that these practices happen all the time, you will create sentiments of disdain towards your kid. This doesn't mean you are an awful parent and it is essential to have apparatuses to react successfully to feelings as they emerge inside our kids and us.

Polyvagal theory and kids

Kids regularly experience issues conveying their sentiments verbally; therefore they much of the time express enthusiastic misery typically. A few kids will, in general, hold enormous sentiments inside. A portion of these kids pull back and abstain from associating with others. Other youngsters are progressively hazardous in nature. These kids may have irate upheavals, pitching sensational fits. In some cases, youngsters are forceful towards other relatives, and others may hurt themselves by pulling out hair or picking at skin. As Parents, these practices can be upsetting to find in kids. However, these practices are additionally techniques that kids use to control their psyche, body, and feelings.

Researches uncover that the elements of the autonomic sensory system are controlled by the vagus nerve in the body. The vagus nerve interfaces the brain to significant frameworks in the body including the stomach and gut, heart, lungs, throat, and facial muscles. Polyvagal theory sets that there are three parts of the vagus nerve; one liable for thoughtful activities, one reaction for parasympathetic activities, and the third, which intervenes and directs the activities of both called the social sensory system. How about we take a gander at these in more noteworthy detail:

- The social sensory system is related to association, tranquility, wellbeing, and attention on the present minute. This segment of the vagus nerve exhausts the face and is found in our children through shimmer in their eyes, a grin on their appearances, and trust in their capacity to move toward the world. The social sensory system is fortified by connections and helps kids effectively explore their thoughtful and parasympathetic sensory systems.

- The thoughtful sensory system is related with high excitement and preparation towards development. In youngsters, you can perceive thoughtful actuation when children are energized, senseless, keyed up, wiggly or squirmy, shocked, irate, on edge, or experience issues dozing. When feeling hazardous or compromised, this shows as a battle or flight reaction. Anyway, when upheld by the social sensory system, this enactment can prepare for the play.

- The parasympathetic sensory system is related to low excitement, unwinding, withdrawal or sadness. At the point when youngsters feel compromised, they may pull back, seem defenseless, and state they are worn out, exhausted, or miserable. Anyway, when upheld by the social sensory system, kids have a sense of security to unwind into an embrace, cuddle with a pet, or wait in calm fulfilling exercises, for example, perusing or drawing.

As Parents, information on the polyvagal theory enables you to help the advancement of the social sensory system in kids to assist them with getting very much adjusted.

Spared by the ball

Here is an individual story that shows the procedure of how we can function with our own feelings to manage our kids:

Following a difficult day, I requested that the children get the toys in the lounge room. Neither one of the children was tuning in. Rather they started squabbling with one another, contending about who made the greater chaos. We were all bad-tempered. I had spent my rationale for the afternoon. I was feeling disappointment ascend inside me. I felt the motivation to holler. I took a full breath, glanced around, and afterward...

the soccer ball made all the difference. Rather than taking my sentiments out on the children, I went to the ball and energetically stated, "Soccer ball, you are not going into the crate! I am so irate with your soccer ball. You are not tuning in to me!" The children and I began chuckling at how senseless it was that I was shouting at the soccer ball and they requested that I do it once more! At that point, they began to tell the different toys that they weren't going on the racks either. We, at that point, cooperated in taking care of the toys, energetically contending with the toys concerning why they expected to head to sleep.

Tools for passionate guideline

The objective of passionate guidelines is to assist kids with realizing that they can have emotions and still be alright, safe, and adored. Here are a few apparatuses I prescribe for when your kid's practices are flagging enthusiastic trouble:

- Do a self-check first: In a plane, you get guidelines to put your breathing device on first; at that point, place it on your youngster. Accept this significant guidance. Ask yourself, would you say you are initiated? What manner of speaking would you say you are utilizing? What is your non-verbal communication conveying? What do you need at the present time? Perhaps you have to extend, inhale, or call somebody who can assist you with feeling progressively associated and safe. On the off chance that your kid's practices are putting themselves or any other individual in danger, by all methods address the worry right away. Yet, in addition, perceive that escaping from your kid is now and then the most ideal approach to protect both yourself and your kid. Self-guideline is testing; be that as it may, rehearsing your techniques before your kid gives important demonstrating. For instance, you may state, "Whew, I am feeling frantic at this moment! I will inhale and step my feet. Ahh, that feels much improved... "
- Become a feeling criminologist: Once you can be increasingly present, watch your kid's practices and be interested in which

sensory system state is predominant. What is their non-verbal communication saying? What methodology is your kid utilizing right presently to oversee feelings? Would you be able to enable your youngster to encounter association? This will help fortify the social sensory system.

- High excitement apparatuses: If your kid is profoundly actuated, investigate meeting them in the high vitality in a steady, fun-loving style. This may include allowing them to push against you while you hold immovably onto a pad or utilizing rich swords to play battle. I generally tell kids that outrage is a solid feeling, and we have to locate a sound method to allow it to out. My child likes to hit a pad while he imparts his irate sentiments to me.
- Low excitement devices: If your kid is pulled back or close down, check whether they will permit you to come right up-front. Utilize your breath and voice tone to impart to your youngster that you give it a second thought. My little girl wants to cover up under a cover when she is overpowered. My activity in those minutes is to smoothly sit by her, just advising her that I am there. In the end, she will twist up on my lap, crucial.

When to look for proficient assistance

At the point when we are stuck in a dynamic with our kids that vibe unfortunate or reliably negative, it is an indication to look for more help. Once in a while, this is a sign to get more prominent comprehension about your kid's practices. On the off chance that your kid has progressing difficulties with sensory, animosity, or withdrawal you don't need to experience this by itself. There are likewise times that looking for more prominent symptomatic clearness is important to manage suitable mediations. Information and aptitudes just take us up until now, particularly when youngsters trigger us as Parents! One of my objectives as an analyst and essayist is to de-trash psycho-treatment. It tends to be lowering and agonizing over requesting help, inspired by a paranoid fear of being judged or seen as a terrible parent. Now and then, getting proficient help for ourselves and our kids is probably the best blessing we can give the people to come.

Are Children Naturally Resilient?

We need to confide in our kids' ability to deal with life's troubles and we would prefer not to over-secure them. In the event that we, as Parents, hop in too rapidly to take care of issues for our kids, we may prevent their capacity to build up their own critical thinking aptitudes. As youngsters figure out how to take care of issues, they build up their ability to be inventive and acknowledge they have an effect on their reality. The world we live in isn't constantly sheltered and kind and we have to have certainty that our kids can eventually deal with this defective world.

In any case, when kids have confronted a mind-boggling life occasion, they regularly need assistance preparing what they have seen and how they feel. At the point when a youngster faces stressors or difficulties, we would prefer not to over-gauge their capacity to deal with it all alone. The result of not supporting kids to process horrible accidents might be lost inventive, scholarly, or social potential.

"In a perfect world, we give youngsters the perfect measure of freedom and challenge offset with adequate help and wellbeing."

Bringing up Resilient Children

Flexibility is our capacity to adjust well even with misfortune; it signifies "bobbing back" from troublesome encounters. As a quality based therapist, I apply to inquire about versatility to my work with kids and families. Caring Adults bring up versatile kids by helping them to comprehend their lives and feel progressively skilled inside their social, passionate, and intellectual advancement.

As Parents, caring emotionally supportive networks assist us with getting to our flexibility so we can enable our youngsters to build up their strength. Versatile kids are sustained via caring Adults who can help them effectively express their experience.

- Younger youngsters may better communicate through play or drawing their involvement in a mindful Adult.
- Older youngsters profit by discussions that reflect feelings, investigate troublesome choices, and inspect the implications kids make about their encounters.

At the point when Children throw you a Curve Ball

Being with a kid who is battling leads most Parents to feel irate or terrified. Particularly when:

- "My kid won't rest or stay unconscious!"
- "My child is forceful and is hitting his more youthful sister or me!"
- "My little girl used to go to class fine and dandy and now she sticks and won't discrete from me when I drop her off for first grade!"
- "My youngster is blocking me out and simply doesn't hear me out!"

Now and then we respond or close down our kids due to our feelings of trepidation and awkward feelings. To need to push our youngsters away or flee from our kids is an ordinary and organically determined reaction when we are apprehensive. Be that as it may, I welcome you to see your kid's "curveballs" as a call to draw in your kid, to look underneath the conduct, and to associate with their inward world. Realizing that you now and then experience outrage when you are defenseless and apprehensive can help you brilliantly turn towards your kid's troublesome practices that emerge out of their vulnerabilities and fears.

Strength is for Parents Too

For Parents, strength permits us to react imaginatively to the difficulties inborn in bringing up our youngsters. Parents need support through merciful associations with accomplices, different Parents, and when fundamental, advisors, to assist us with investigating the more profound topics of responses to youngsters and how this might be associated with the past. Being a strong parent

Implies:

- Getting backing to gain from your deterrents so you can bolster your kids to gain from their battles.
- Accepting that you are blemished so you can be kinder towards your kids' errors.
- Recognizing that you don't have all the appropriate responses with the goal that you are additionally tolerating when kids feel lost or befuddled.
- Remembering that you like being adored and known for what your identity is so you can expect to love and know your youngsters for what their identity is.

On a plane, they will consistently advise the Adults to put their breathing apparatus on first – at that point, help your youngster to put theirs on. The equivalent is valid with versatility: When Adults feel bolstered they are better ready to help their kids.

Strength Informed Treatment

As individuals, we would all be able to get "stuck" in some cases. There is no compelling reason to feel embarrassed or humiliated to request help, whether it is for yourself or your youngster. Flexibility educated treatment perceives that when Parents and youngsters have a sense of security and bolstered you can get to your innovativeness, quality, and ability to deal with life's difficulties.

CHAPTER FIVE:
POLYVAGAL THEORY AND ANXIETY

Polyvagal Theory may give inventive intercessions to both tension and wretchedness. Numerous individuals become caught in ruminating about the past or agonizing over the future; they can't appear to keep their brain and body right now. Some solid, dread based, real resistances may not react well to "talk treatment" alone. In helping customers with such enduring, it is critical to incorporate an exceptionally solid clinical collusion and relationship, just as close to home story on interior introjected messages about their vulnerabilities, fears, and self-questions. Review that uneasiness is commonly a body-based safeguard from lower brain territories (limbic and mind stem). These territories are regularly un-influenced when simply "talk" happens in treatment. There are sure signs that an individual's tension is misbehaving in a clinical meeting. These are:

- Higher pitched voice, now and then with quick conveyance;
- Prolonged hushes;
- Tighter, level face and tight jaw – regularly with the upper cosmetic touch-ups marginally;
- Random apprehensive body developments;
- Rapid, higher-chest relaxing;
- Problems in mindfulness, memory, and subjective appreciation; and,
- Sometimes out and out frenzy.

At the point when such restless resistances show up, the advisor needs to move to establish and quiet breathing mediations. Talking it through, working it through might be lacking to reestablish feeling guidelines. It is recommended to initiate polyvagal impedance to uneasiness. In the event that effective, feeling guidelines will be restored.

- Request the customer to breathe out more gradually, and with more accentuation.

- Then have the individual expand their exhalation marginally. Be mindful so as not to expand excessively far; inconvenience will follow.
- If the individual is frightful of open talking or introducing in a gathering treatment meeting, demand that they add more words to their sentences. This will require an adjustment in breathing procedure – consequently expanding the exhalation.
- Practice longer exhalations as the customer inhales all the more gradually and all the more profoundly.
- Have the customer lay on their back with their marginally bowed legs high up on a divider – relax

At the point when your body encounters uneasiness, it does what it's prepared to do: respond to the condition of dread you're detecting.

As Stephen Porges says, "Uneasiness is our higher mind structures deciphering a substantial (lower brain) reaction as requiring a guard."

In case you're acquainted with uneasiness or stress, you realize the heart dashing, chest-beating and real dread that ascents like a flee lift in your body. It can forget about you lashing with fury and outrage or leaving your prompt condition as everything whirls into an awkward blend of overpowering.

Instructing yourself to unwind once in a while works

Tuning in to other people who let you know not to stress seldom works either.

How Your Body Responds To Stress and Anxiety

At the point when your mind detects fear, it actuates your thoughtful sensory system. Everything alerts, alarms and glimmering lights are making your body aware of threat ... regardless of whether the 'risk' is by and large late for a significant gathering, contending with your accomplice, or attempting to make it to take a shot at time subsequent to managing an agitated youngster.

At the point when these alerts go off you'll see these physiological changes as blood is coordinated to parts of the body important to deal with the apparent threat:

- You're breathing shifts more into the upper piece of your chest
- Your breaths become shorter
- Your pulse rises
- Your muscles become progressively tense
- The upper piece of your face becomes compliment or has less appearance
- Your voice turns out to be all the more piercing with a smaller scope of pitch

When the risk is over your body's parasympathetic sensory system restores your body to its harmony. Furthermore, life goes on ... until the following upsetting occasion happens - OR the pressure you're encountering in your life is all inescapable and accordingly is keeping your body on high alarm in any event when there is no 'activating' occurrence for you to feel on edge.

Why Your Personal Narrative Adds To The Problem

As your body moves into an on edge state, what you enlighten yourself concerns the importance behind the inclination matters.

For instance, you might be:

- Telling yourself that you're dreadful of getting into a lift, an airplane or a room without windows as it triggers considerations of a past horrible mishap
- Avoiding swarmed places or boisterous situations as they trigger overpower
- Hearing your internal identity recommend things that could not be right in the event that you see your chief/supervisor strolling towards you (for example I've committed an error, I'll be sacked, somebody's griped about me, I've been late for gatherings)
- Noticing your child or little child waking and feeling overpowered

at adapting to their vitality level, crying or not having the opportunity to finish the horde of things you have to do.
- Having dreams that wake you making you feel as though you're having a wellbeing emergency

These individual stories might be driving you to feel excessively incredulous of yourself, accusing yourself, feeling a feeling of disgrace or making a decision about yourself as basically 'not sufficient'.

Passionate states activated by tension are not intentional; they're customized from a transformative point of view. Your brain is ensuring you such that's protected warm-blooded creatures from the most punctual of times - it's a programmed reaction exuding from the most established piece of your mind - frequently called the reptilian mind.

Once 'risk' is felt, those 'on edge' reactions swell all through your body - implying that if your heart begins beating different pieces of your body (lungs, gut, muscles) will likewise 'get the dread message' and react.

In the event that you can figure out how to change one part of this automatic gradually expanding influence, at that point, it's conceivable to restore the body back to quiet more rapidly.

While it's not all that simple to slow your pulse (except if you're a rehearsed meditator) you can deal with your relaxing.

This is the reason why this method is basic, yet so compelling

To change your physiological state so you have a progressively positive, controlled and fitting reaction, it is recommended: controlling your breath.

While this method depends on conventional breathing activities, he makes it one stride further by presenting 'deceiving' your psyche into easing back you are relaxing.

He says: When you're encountering pressure, your hands and chest might be fixing. You're breathing from a higher point in your chest. Furthermore, these body reactions are making a physiological expression that underpins the sentiment of sensoryness.

Right now, the brain isn't preparing the coherent answer of 'simply unwind' on the grounds that you're encapsulating uneasiness and not taking in the meaningful gestures that could ease on edge sentiments.

While encountering a condition of pressure or tension, higher-request thinking gets restricted. In the event that somebody is encountering sensoryness, they may confuse an individual with an 'unbiased' demeanor all over as being undermining or potentially judgemental.

So figuring out how to oversee tension at the time is a significant aptitude to ace as your 'legitimate mind' can't bolster you in the manner in which it ordinarily does.

Breathing Technique:

Utilize this method to 'stunt' yourself into hindering your relaxing.

Breath out gradually by expanding the term of your expressions - for example: saying more words before slowly inhaling. He says that numerous individuals encountering tension change their discourse example and slowly inhale on each other word, so by taking more time to breathe out, you'll help your body's parasympathetic reaction (the piece of your autonomic framework that urges you to rest and unwind).

This is an incredible tip in case you're going to introduce at a gathering or give a discussion and need to quiet the nerves; however, shouldn't something be said about the ordinary circumstance?

An Every Day Breathing Technique You Can Use Anywhere

I like to utilize a comparative methodology, yet with an increasingly programmed technique - tallying.

It includes tallying in reverse from ten to one.

As you start, say the word 'ten' as gradually as possible, discharging your breath completely.

Presently take an ordinary breath in.

Now proceed with 'nine', saying it as gradually as you can and discharging your breath completely.

Proceed right now you reach 'one' - notice the distinction in your chest, gut region, shoulders, hands, facial muscles, throat and leg muscles.

Elective: For each number, picture the relating measure of candles. As you state each number, picture smothering the candles in a gradual breathe out. This diverts you from the wellspring of tension, so you center more on your breathing and extinguishing the candles.

CHAPTER SIX:
POLYVAGAL THEORY AND PTSD

One of the difficult repercussions of Post-Traumatic Stress Disorder (PTSD) is the experience of an absence of control that can happen when you feel caught by sentiments of sensoryness, alarm, overpower, or despair. Polyvagal theory, offers a significant system for comprehension and adequately reacting to the extraordinary passionate and physiological manifestations of PTSD.

"Mending the sensory system can require some investment and requires persistence. Put the polyvagal theory without hesitation in your life to expand your feeling of opportunity in body and brain" - Dr. Arielle Schwartz

The Sensory System: A Basic Model

An essential model of the sensory system shows that we have two segments of our sensory system, one that is under our cognizant control (for example moving your hand) and another that capacities without our mindfulness (for example controlling our internal heat level), the segment of the sensory system that capacity without our cognizant mindfulness is known as the autonomic sensory system (ANS). The entirety of our enthusiastic articulations are interceded by the ANS as it either activates vitality through our thoughtful sensory system or rations vitality through our parasympathetic sensory system.

- The thoughtful sensory system is related to the battle or flight reaction and the arrival of cortisol (stress synthetic substances) all through the circulatory system.
- The parasympathetic is related to unwinding, processing, and recovery.

The thoughtful and parasympathetic sensory systems are intended to work in a cadenced shift that underpins sound absorption, rest, and resistant framework working.

Modern researches offer a propelled comprehension of the ANS, particularly as identified with injury and PTSD. The autonomic sensory system is directed by the vagus nerve or the tenth cranial nerve. The vagus nerve interfaces the brain to significant frameworks in the body, supporting psyche body correspondences.

Warm-blooded animals have two vagal circuits, a developmentally more established circuit called the dorsal vagal intricate and an all the more as of late advanced vagal circuit called the "ventral vagal complex" (VVC) which is additionally alluded to as the "social sensory system." The dorsal vagal complex interfaces with the organs underneath the stomach, including the spleen, liver, kidneys, just as the little and internal organs. The ventral vagal, social sensory system interfaces over the stomach to your heart, lungs, larynx, pharynx, internal ear, just as the facial muscles around your mouth and eyes.

Extensively, the vagus nerve is constantly connected with the parasympathetic sensory system and has an inhibitory impact upon the heart and thoughtful sensory system movement. In particular, deeper examinations recognized that the parasympathetic sensory system has two introductions that rely on whether you have a sense of security or feel compromised. In the midst of security, the parasympathetic sensory system encourages rest, unwinding, and processing. In any case, in the midst of danger, the parasympathetic sensory system has a protective mode.

Bioconductal Defenses

At the point when we feel compromised, we will commonly endeavor to draw in the social sensory system to restore a feeling of association and security. On the off chance that we can't make protected, social security, we will logically fall back on developmentally more established bioconductal resistance techniques. In the first place, we will draw upon thoughtful sensory system activities, for example, battle or trip to prepare us into self-security. Here, you may feel temperamental, on edge, or panicky.

On the off chance that the thoughtful sensory system is ineffective in re-establishing security, we will default to the developmentally most seasoned piece of the vagus nerve, the "dorsal vagal complex" (DVC). This increasingly crude technique connects with the parasympathetic sensory system in a foul way. Here, the parasympathetic sensory system connects with immobilizing cautious procedures, for example, separation or blacking out. Here, you may feel worn out, dazed, or sick.

The Vagal Brake

Both the dorsal vagal complex (DVC) and the ventral vagal complex (VVC) will apply hindrance to the thoughtful sensory system. The Polyvagal Theory utilizes an analogy proposing that the vagus nerve resembles squeezing the brake pedal when driving a vehicle. Expulsion of the parasympathetic "vagal brake" causes an expansion in pulse and more prominent helplessness to push.

The social sensory system works as a refined brake, which has quieting and alleviating impacts reflected in musical motions in pulse fluctuation. This is related to increments in wellbeing and enthusiastic prosperity. Conversely, the dorsal vagal complex acts as a sudden vagal brake. Stalling out right now a protective technique for significant stretches of time can have genuine repercussions on mental and physical wellbeing.

The Social Sensory System

Your social sensory system (VVC) is reinforced by myelination. Myelination is a greasy covering on nerve pathways that are expanded through rehashed use and results in speed up and control. You can envision here the myelination that happens in the learning of another bit of music for the piano. At first, notes are played gradually and cautiously; however, with rehashed practice, you start to make music, in the end without perusing the music by any stretch of the imagination. In like manner, the pathways of the social sensory system are reinforced through rehashed practice. You realize that you are in your social sensory system when you feel a glow in your grin and see the radiance in your eyes. You can draw in your social sensory system to associate with others, feel fun-loving, and unwind into an association. On the off chance that you feel pointlessly keyed up with tension, you can utilize the social sensory system to distinguish that you are protected. You can glance around and tune in for signals of wellbeing or participate in systems, for example, quiet, slow breathing to enable you to unwind. These activities utilize the activity frameworks over the stomach.

When you realize that you are protected, you never again need to concentrate outward. This permits you to interface with the helpful side of your Dorsal Vagal Complex. Here, you can decide to immobilize into an encounter of security by unwinding into an embrace with a friend or family member or resting into a sustaining contemplation. It is additionally conceivable to mix your social sensory system with your thoughtful sensory system, which encourages your capacity to participate in a vivacious play. Your social sensory system expands your capacity to react successfully when you grope keyed with tension or shut-down with melancholy.

Activation into Play – Immobilization into Intimacy

Regardless of whether you are feeling uneasiness or melancholy, you can utilize instruments to draw in your social sensory system to restore higher request sensory system capacities.

On the off chance that you are encountering tension, you are likely in battle or flight, a key protection response of the thoughtful sensory system. Thoughtful activities include activation; the need to move your body to discharge the work of pressure cortisols. You can draw in your social apprehensive by scouring your hands together overwhelmingly and reaching to your own face, neck, upper chest, arms, and legs. You can likewise investigate physical developments that vibe safe and establishing, for example, taking a walk or shaking your arms and legs to discharge pressure. At the point when we have a sense of security, we can connect with our social sensory system to utilize the vitality of the thoughtful sensory system to move, play, and giggle.

Feeling shut down, crumbled, discouraged, or numb means that you are in the cautious responses of your parasympathetic sensory system which is portrayed by immobilization. In the event that you have a background marked by injury, it is conceivable that you are seeing dangers in your condition that are not really happening in the present time and place. This is on the grounds that a typical indication of PTSD is disarray between the past and the present. Right now, the social sensory system can help perceive that you are not in fast approaching peril. This permits you to get to the positive, loosening up components of your parasympathetic sensory system to "rest and review." When conceivable, turn towards a caring association with a companion, caring accomplice, or a pet. At first, you may need to look or call somebody you trust and tune in to the sound of their voice. You can likewise imagine a caring creature, companion, or defensive partner to reestablish a felt feeling of association. At the point when you can grasp immobilization with security, you can get to the sustenance of the unwinding reaction.

Suggestions for Healing PTSD

The polyvagal theory in real life can permit you to expand your feeling of opportunity in body and brain while encountering manifestations of tension, frenzy, or sadness. Here are a few recommendations:

- Focus on the present minute
- Engage the feeling of smell with basic oil that brings a positive affiliation or feeling
- Re-set up association by calling a companion, cuddling with your pet, or cherishing self-touch
- Express emotions through talking, composing, drawing, or development

- Focus on your breath as a calibrating instrument to control the sensory system
- Engage in care practice, for example, reflection or remedial yoga
- Allow yourself to play or get innovative
- Focus on the great by tuning into the magnificence around you

Restorative ramifications of Polyvagal Theory educate Somatic brain science and EMDR Treatment. Recuperating the sensory system can require some serious energy and requires persistence with the procedure and with yourself. You are not bombing when you feel on edge or discouraged. You are additionally not the only one. Put the polyvagal theory vigorously in your life to build your feeling of opportunity in the body and brain. Further Reading:

Recuperating from Developmental Trauma

Awful encounters are, by their very definition, terrifying and overpowering. Occasions such as auto collisions, catastrophic events, or demonstrations of brutality, change our natural direction to the world. It isn't unexpected to feel overflowed with incredible feelings, sensations, or recollections as we adjust to new and frequently undesirable reality. Some of the time we begin to maintain a strategic distance from places suggestive of the injury. Or on the other hand, we may have or have nosy recollections and emotions. Post-Traumatic Stress Disorder (PTSD) alludes to the nearness of these indications well after the occasion is finished. Nonetheless, Complex PTSD and separation is another sort of post awful pressure. At the point when you experience youth disregard or constant maltreatment, your essential direction to the world is one of danger, dread, and endurance. Deceitful Parents or parental figures leave you untrusting or befuddled about what comprises a caring relationship. Dread and absence of security leaves you checking your condition for potential dangers. An ignored or mishandled kid will depend upon worked in, organic assurance components for endurance to "block out" the risk. Examples of dread and separation advise the creating body and psyche.

"Adults mishandled as youngsters frequently report feeling vulnerable, sad, despair, profound dejection, disgrace, shamefulness, bad form, clearing discouragement, and self-destructive musings. Many keep on pushing the unnerving, yucky, difficult, and confounding emotions far away by turning to learned dissociative examples. Despite the fact that you are protected now, it can feel overpowering to recognize leftovers of verifiable dangers held in the body, feelings, and brain. We mend early formative injury inside a protected relationship that is conscious, unsurprising, predictable, non-guarded and has clear limits. Delicately we rethink our ability for a relationship with a dependable other. Gradually we reconstruct confidence in ourselves."

Separation and Defenses

Kids require consistency and normality with parental figures so they can grow clear assumptions regarding themselves and the world. Such steadiness gives the ground of security and permits kids to adjust to the internal changes that normally happen during early improvement. When stood up to with a perilous and unusual condition, babies and youngsters block out and go off to endure. Separation turns into a very much kept up division between the piece of oneself engaged with staying aware of everyday undertakings of living and those parts that are holding the feelings of dread, disgrace, or outrage.

Dissociative side effects can be generally mellow, for example, feeling foggy or fluffy, making some hard memories discussing encounters, feeling mixed up, and feeling tired. Increasingly extreme side effects incorporate inclination "crazy," having breaches of memory, or reports of "lost time." In the most serious circumstances of Dissociative Identity Disorder, it is conceivable to build up various parts with unmistakable sub-characters.

Complex PTSD and separation are kept up by barriers, for example, refusal, constraint, romanticizing, or minimization of the past. Or then again, we use substances or keep up other addictive practices to abstain from feeling the agony. Here are a few models:

- "Yeah, he was an abuser; however, it is anything but a serious deal."
- "They were awesome Parents; however, they celebrated a great deal and I was left to raise myself a significant part of the time."
- "It's simply an excessive amount to recognize what occurred."
- "Why feel when I can… eat, drink, smoke pot, take a valium, and so on."

Settling Complex PTSD and Dissociation

Horrendous examples will, in general, be remembered and re-sanctioned. Despite the fact that they are agonizing, horrendous examples are commonplace; giving up can really feel additionally overpowering. It can feel more secure not to confide in individuals. It can feel simpler not to change.

Social psycho-treatment with a clinician educated about a formative injury can help. Suggested modalities incorporate EMDR Treatment and Somatic Treatment (body-focused). Scientists propose that the recuperating of early formative injury must happen inside a sheltered relationship that is aware, unsurprising, reliable, non-protective, and that has clear limits. The way toward mending complex PTSD includes:

- Observing your examples of separation.
- Accepting and adoring yourself with the entirety of your barriers.
- Compassionately perceiving the effect of separation on your life and connections today.
- Recognizing that an awful accident transpired.
- Realizing that expanded mindfulness brings expanded decision.
- Increasing resilience for dismissal, misfortune, disillusionment, disgrace, strife, and vulnerability.
- Decreasing the dependence upon guards that keep up a separation from difficult sentiments.
- Recognizing that the startling or risky occasions are over at this

point.
- Distinguishing between the over a wide span of time all the more unmistakably.
- Reclaiming adaptability in your body and psyche.
- Developing new, solid assumptions regarding connections.
- Having an away from the effect of social injuries experienced in youth develops empathy.

Developing Compassion

Regardless of whether you are a customer, a clinician, a mindful companion, or an accomplice, having an away from the effect of youth social injury develops sympathy. Adults manhandled as kids can feel vulnerability, misery, despair, profound forlornness, disgrace, shamefulness, bad form, clearing despondency, and self-destructive musings. Many keep on pushing the alarming, yucky, difficult, and befuddling emotions far away by turning to learned dissociative examples.

Numerous individuals with a background marked by complex PTSD and separation have been misconstrued, misdiagnosed, and over-cured. Shockingly, good-natured care-suppliers can accept that side effects are the aftereffect of a shortcoming of character; a harming outcome that "accuses the person in question" and meddles with recuperating.

Despite the fact that there might be security now, it can even now feel overpowering to recognize the remainders of chronicled dangers held in body, feelings, and brain. Tenderly recuperating happens in a relationship with a reliable other. Gradually we revamp confidence in ourselves.

CHAPTER SEVEN:
THE VAGAL PARADOX

The gauge of vagal tone got from estimating respiratory sinus arrhythmia, could be utilized in clinical medicine as a record of pressure defenselessness. Instead of utilizing the engaging proportions of pulse changeability (i.e., beat-to-thump fluctuation) as often as possible utilized in obstetrics and pediatrics, the paper underlined that respiratory sinus arrhythmia has neural inception and speaks to the tonic utilitarian outpouring from the vagus to the heart (i.e., cardiovascular vagal tone). Along these lines, it was recommended that respiratory sinus arrhythmia would give a more delicate file of wellbeing status than an increasingly worldwide proportion of beat-to-thump pulse fluctuation reflecting unsure neural and nonneural systems.

The paper introduced a quantitative methodology that applied time-arrangement investigations to separate the abundancy of respiratory sinus arrhythmia as a progressively exact list of vagal action. The article gave information showing that sound full-term newborn children had respiratory sinus arrhythmia of essentially more noteworthy abundancy than did preterm babies. This thought of utilizing pulse examples to record vagal action was not new, having been accounted for as right on time as 1910 by Hering.5 Moreover, contemporary examinations have dependably detailed that vagal bar through atropine discourages respiratory sinus arrhythmia in warm-blooded animals.

A neonatologist, as a clinical understudy, discovered that vagal tone could be deadly. He contended that might be an overdose of something that is otherwise good (i.e., vagal tone) could be terrible. He was alluding, obviously, to the clinical danger of neurogenic bradycardia. Bradycardia, when seen during conveyance, might be a pointer of fetal misery. Thus, bradycardia and apnea are significant pointers of hazard for the infant.

Further examination were done on this bewildering perception by considering the human baby during conveyance. Fetal bradycardia happened just when respiratory sinus arrhythmia was discouraged (i.e., a respiratory beat in the fetal pulse is perceptible even without the enormous chest divider developments related to breathing that happen postpartum). This brought up the issue of how vagal instruments could intercede both respiratory sinus arrhythmia and bradycardia, as one is defensive and the other is conceivably deadly. This irregularity turned into the "vagal oddity" and filled in as the inspiration driving the polyvagal theory.

With respect to the instruments intervening bradycardia and pulse inconstancy, there is a conspicuous irregularity among information and physiological suspicions. Physiological models expect vagal guidelines of both chronotropic control of the heart (i.e., pulse) and the abundancy of respiratory sinus arrhythmia. For instance, it has been dependably detailed that vagal cardio-inhibitory filaments to the heart have steady utilitarian properties portrayed by bradycardia to neural incitement and respiratory rhythm.9 However, despite the fact that there are circumstances where the two measures covary (e.g., during exercise and cholinergic barricade), there are different circumstances in which the measures seem to reflect autonomous wellsprings of neural control (e.g., bradycardic scenes related with hypoxia, vasovagal syncope, and fetal trouble). As opposed to these detectable marvels, scientists keep on arguing for covariation between these two parameters. This irregularity, in light of a suspicion of a solitary focal vagal source, is the thing that I have marked the vagal Catch.

Examination of the phylogeny of the vertebrate autonomic sensory system gives a response to the vagal Catch. Research in near neuroanatomy and neurophysiology has distinguished two parts of the vagus, with each branch supporting distinctive versatile capacities and social systems. The vagal yield to the heart from one branch is showed in respiratory sinus arrhythmia, and the yield from the other branch is showed in bradycardia and perhaps the more slow rhythms in pulse changeability. In spite of the fact that the more slow rhythms have been expected to have a thoughtful impact, they are obstructed by atropine.

The polyvagal theory, explains how every one of three phylogenetic stages in the improvement of the vertebrate autonomic sensory system is related to a particular autonomic subsystem that is held and communicated in warm-blooded creatures. These autonomic subsystems are phylogenetically requested and typically connected to social correspondence (e.g., outward appearance, vocalization, tuning in), assembly (e.g., battle flight practices), and immobilization (e.g., faking passing, vasovagal syncope, and conduct shutdown).

The social correspondence framework (i.e., social commitment framework; see underneath) includes the myelinated vagus, which serves to encourage quiet conduct states by restraining thoughtful impacts to the heart and hosing the hypothalamic-pituitary-adrenal (HPA) axis. The assembly framework is subject to the working of the thoughtful sensory system. The most phylo-hereditarily crude segment, the immobilization framework, is subject to the unmyelinated vagus, which is imparted to most vertebrates. With expanded neural unpredictability coming about because of phylogenetic improvement, the creature's conduct and full of feeling collection is advanced. The three circuits can be conceptualized as unique, giving versatile reactions to sheltered, hazardous, and dangerous occasions and settings.

Just warm-blooded creatures have a myelinated vagus. In contrast to the unmyelinated vagus, starting in the dorsal engine core of the vagus with pre-and postganglionic muscarinic receptors, the mammalian myelinated vagus begins in the core ambiguous and has preganglionic nicotinic receptors and postganglionic muscarinic receptors. The unmyelinated vagus is imparted to different vertebrates, including reptiles, creatures of land and water, teleosts, and elasmobranchs.

We are presently examining the chance of extricating various highlights of the pulse example to progressively screen the two vagal frameworks. Starter concentrates in our research center to help this chance. In these investigations, we have hindered the nicotinic preganglionic receptors with hexamethonium and the muscarinic receptors with atropine. The information was gathered from the prairie vole, which has a high surrounding vagal tone. This primer information showed that, in a few creatures, nicotinic bar specifically evacuates respiratory sinus arrhythmia without hosing the adequacy of the lower frequencies in pulse inconstancy. Conversely, hindering the muscarinic receptors with atropine evacuates both the low and respiratory frequencies.

Consistency with Jacksonian Dissolution

The three circuits are sorted out and react to difficulties in a phylogenetically decided chain of importance reliable with the Jacksonian standard of disintegration. Jackson suggested that in the brain, higher (i.e., phylogenetically more up to date) neural circuits hinder lower (i.e., phylogenetically more seasoned) neural circuits and "when the higher are unexpectedly rendered functionless, the lower ascend in activity." Although Jackson proposed disintegration to clarify changes in mind work because of harm and ailment, the polyvagal theory proposes a comparable phylogenetically requested various leveled model to portray the grouping of autonomic reaction systems to challenges.

Practically, when nature is seen as protected, two significant highlights are communicated. Real state is controlled in a proficient way to advance development and reclamation (e.g., instinctive homeostasis). This is done through an expansion in the impact of mammalian myelinated vagal engine pathways on the cardiovascular pacemaker that eases back the heart, restrains the battle flight instruments of the thoughtful sensory system, hoses the pressure reaction arrangement of the HPA pivot (e.g., cortisol), and decreases aggravation by balancing resistant responses (e.g., cytokines). Second, through the procedure of development, the brainstem cores that manage the myelinated vagus got incorporated with the cores that direct the muscles of the face and head.

This connection brings about the bidirectional coupling between unconstrained social commitment practices and real states. In particular, an incorporated social commitment framework developed in warm-blooded animals when the neural guideline of instinctive states that advance development and reclamation (by means of the myelinated vagus) was connected neuroanatomically and neurophysiologically with the neural guideline of the muscles controlling eye stare, outward appearance, tuning in, and prosody.

The human sensory system, like that of different warm-blooded animals, developed not exclusively to make due in safe conditions yet additionally to advance endurance in perilous and dangerous settings. To achieve this versatile adaptability, the human sensory system held two progressively crude neural circuits to manage guarded techniques (i.e., battle flight and passing pretending practices). Note that social conduct, social correspondence, and instinctive homeostasis are contradictory to the neurophysiological states and practices advanced by the two neural circuits that help barrier systems. Therefore, by means of advancement, the human sensory system holds three neural circuits, which are in a phylogenetically sorted out chain of command. Right now, versatile reactions, the most up to date circuit is utilized first; if that circuit neglects to give wellbeing, the more established circuits are selected successively.

Examination of the phylogeny of the vertebrate heart has prompted extraction of four rules that give a premise to testing of speculations relating specific neural components to social commitment, battle flight, and passing pretending practices:

- There is a phylogenetic move in the guideline of the heart from endocrine correspondence to unmyelinated nerves, lastly to myelinated nerves.
- There is an advancement of contradicting neural components of excitation and restraint to give a fast guideline of evaluated metabolic yield.
- A face - heart association developed as source cores of vagal pathways moved ventrally from the more established dorsal engine core to the core ambiguous. This brought about an anatomical and neurophysiological linkage between neural

guidelines of the heart by means of the myelinated vagus and the exceptional instinctive efferent pathways that control the striated muscles of the face and head, framing an incorporated social commitment framework.

- With expanded cortical improvement, the cortex shows more noteworthy power over the brainstem by means of direct (e.g., corticobulbar) and backhanded (e.g., corticoreticular) neural pathways beginning in engine cortex and ending in the source cores of the myelinated engine nerves rising up out of the brainstem (e.g., specific neural pathways inserted inside cranial nerves V, VII, IX, X, and XI), controlling visceromotor structures (i.e., heart, bronchi) just as somatomotor structures (muscles of the face and head).

Neuroception: Contextual Cueing of Adaptive, Maladaptive Physiological States

Too successfully change from guarded to social commitment methodologies, the mammalian sensory system needs to perform two significant versatile errands:

- Valuate hazard, and
- If the earth is seen as protected, hinder the more crude limbic structures that control battle, flight, or freeze practices.

Any boost that has the potential for expanding a creature's understanding of security has the capability of selecting the developmentally further developed neural circuits that help the prosocial practices of the social commitment framework. The sensory system, through the handling of tactile data from nature and from the viscera, consistently assesses hazards. Since the neural assessment of hazard doesn't require cognizant mindfulness and may include subcortical limbic structures, the term neuroception22 was acquainted with stress a neural procedure, particularly from observation, that is equipped for recognizing ecological (and instinctive) highlights that are sheltered, hazardous, or perilous. In save situations, the autonomic state is adaptively managed to hose thoughtful actuation and to ensure the oxygen-subordinate focal sensory system, particularly the cortex, from the metabolic traditionalist responses of the dorsal vagal complex. In any case, how does the sensory system know when the earth is sheltered, perilous, or hazardous, and which neural instruments assess this hazard?

Ecological segments of neuroception

Neuroception speaks to a neural procedure that empowers people and different warm-blooded animals to participate in social practices by recognizing safe from hazardous settings. Neuroception is proposed as a conceivable component intervening both the demeanor and the disturbance of positive social conduct, feeling guideline, and instinctive homeostasis. Neuroception may be activated by include finders including regions of the worldly cortex that speak with the focal core of the amygdala and the periaqueductal dark since limbic reactivity is tweaked by fleeting cortex reactions to the expectation of voices, faces, and hand developments. In this manner, the neuroception of comfortable people and people with suitably prosodic voices and warm, expressive appearances converts into social communication advancing a feeling of security.In many people (i.e., those without a mental issue or neuropathology), the sensory system assesses risks and matches the neurophysiological state with the genuine danger of the earth. At the point when nature is assessed as being sheltered, the guarded limbic structures are restrained, empowering social commitment and quiet instinctive states to develop. Interestingly, a few people experience befuddle and the sensory system assesses nature as being hazardous in any event, when it is protected. This befuddle brings about physiological states that help battle, flight, or freeze practices, yet not social commitment practices. As per the theory, social correspondence can be communicated effectively through the social commitment framework just when these protective circuits are restrained.

Different supporters of neuroception

The highlights of hazard in nature don't exclusively drive neuroception. Afferent input from the viscera gives a significant middle person of the availability of prosocial circuits related to social commitment practices. For instance, the polyvagal theory predicts that conditions of the assembly would bargain with our capacity to distinguish positive expressive gestures. Practically, instinctive states shading our view of articles and others. In this way, similar highlights of one individual drawing in another may bring about a scope of results, contingent upon the physiological condition of the objective person. In the event that the individual being locked in will be in a state wherein the social commitment framework is effectively available, equal prosocial collaborations are probably going to happen. Be that as it may, if the individual is in a condition of preparation, the equivalent drawing accordingly may be reacted to with the asocial highlights of withdrawal or animosity. In such a state, it may be hard to hose the preparation circuit and empower the social commitment framework to return online.

The insula might be associated with the intervention of neuroception since it has been proposed as a mind structure engaged with passing on the diffuse criticism from the viscera into cognitive-mindfulness. Utilitarian imaging tests have exhibited that the insula assumes a significant job in the experience of agony and the experience of a few feelings, including outrage, dread, disturb, bliss, and pity. Critchley suggests that interior body states are spoken to in the insula and add to conditions of emotional inclination, and he has exhibited that action in the insula connects with interoceptive exactness.

CHAPTER EIGHT:
DORSAL VAGAL, FREEZE, AND POLYVAGAL SOLUTIONS

As we talked about in the previous chapter, the essential job of the dorsal vagal framework, in people, is to manage organs beneath the stomach. In any case, that is by all accounts, not the only job. We should place it in context. Hereditarily, the dorsal vagal pathway of the autonomic sensory system is fundamentally the same as what's been seen in hard fish and even cartilaginous fish. When it developed to warm-blooded animals, its job was truly consigned fundamentally to beneath the stomach.

This implies it manages essentially every one of those instinctive organs that we are truly not mindful of. In any case, there are a few tracks, or pathways, that are still, as it were minimal, old frameworks that go to the heart and to zones like the throat. If you somehow managed to animate the uttermost, most profound piece of your throat, that would be controlled by the dorsal vagus. Obviously, what occurs in the event that you invigorate that piece of the throat? You disgorge

Disgorging is, one might say is a dorsal vagal reaction. The framework is truly going down and this is a versatile methodology for disposing of poisons and different things that might be happening. In any case, when we talk about the dorsal vagal framework it begins in the mind stem region called the dorsal engine core of the vagus or all the more generally now known as the dorsal core of the vagus.

A portion of the pathways really relocate through the core questionable and afterward return through the vagus and a portion of those that moved really wind up being a piece of the core equivocal or the ventral vagus. When you see it originating from the brain stem, you essentially have a bound together coordinated nerve. Many individuals feel that they're two separate nerves, the ventral vagus and the dorsal vagus; nonetheless, they're actually across the board conductor and we need to imagine that.

There are just about 15% of the filaments in that course. 15% to 20% of those strands are really efferent filaments significance going down from the mind. Of that 15%, really 80% of those are heading off to the dorsal vagus, and not many are setting off to the ventral vagus. So extremely, the prevalent highlights of our vagal framework are really managing sub-diaphragmatic organs. The significant part that we truly need to get to when we start talking about pain is this job of the afferents of these frameworks, being the tangible part returning to the mind. So the dorsal vagus originates from a territory that is dorsal to the core uncertain.

The Role of the Dorsal Vagal and Pain

Holding those particular subtleties is truly not significant in light of the fact that they're extremely insignificant to understanding the capacity. The capacity that we start understanding is that the core ambiguous vagal filaments are connected with the face and influence that we ordinarily have, while the dorsal vagal strands are all the more overwhelmingly connected to regions underneath the stomach. Gastric torments, touchy inside, every one of these things that are truly manifestations of different disorders that numerous individuals who endure injury has, are truly pointers of an atypical guideline of the dorsal vagus.

This turns out to be extremely significant in light of the fact that inside the model of the Polyvagal Theory, both the thoughtful sensory system and the dorsal vagus can be enlisted as protection frameworks. At the point when the ventral vagus is truly working at an elevated level and managing great, at that point, the sympathetic are simply part of the homeostatic procedures. They bolster wellbeing, development, and rebuilding. They additionally bolster development without being a protection framework.

Significance of Ventral Vagal Activity to avert Defense and Shutdown

So also a similar analogy works for the dorsal vagus. The dorsal vagus is basic; it is anything but an awful framework; however, it's not beneficial for that framework to be utilized or enlisted as a safeguard. That turns out to be extremely, the essential issue and the Polyvagal Theory gives you the various leveled model. It says, as long as the ventral vagus is truly in direction or running, at that point, your sympathetic can move any way they need in a progressively homeostatic manner to advance bloodstream and advance solid development and reclamation. It's just when the ventral vagus gets withdrawn that we get into this helplessness of a thoughtful safeguard framework. At the point when that doesn't work well, the dorsal vagus is the main thing you have left and that closes you down. You start seeing the progressive way that things work.

What is extremely significant is the job of the vagal afferents from the gut, from the sub stomach. Their job in the tweak of agony is a piece of this present part's accentuation. Diminish noticed the way that the vegas nerve, the biggest nerve in the entire human body is 80% afferent, when we see what happens when individuals stall out in the dorsal vagal framework. Steve has underlined its administrative capacity, both the dorsal vagal and the thoughtful, and obviously the ventral vagal. Yet, there are numerous circumstances, especially injury and agony - where this guideline isn't generally homeostatic, where it's maladaptive.

Methodologies to Shift out of Maladaptive Defense States

One of the manners in which that we can change out of those maladaptive states, because of injury or pain, is through invigorating these afferents. There are a few different ways - one, for instance, is the utilization, for instance, of vibrating a sound, directly from the instinctive zone where you appear to be animating those afferents. At times you'll see an individual go from shut down and into harmony. Thoughtful hyper excitement is an integral part of this substantial autonomic example of supporting, of choking, of holding. This prompts torment and that torment itself brings on additional propping and further actuation of the thoughtful framework. At the point when the supporting example and the torment itself have become increasingly intense, the body closes down additional into what Steve has discussed as a metabolic retreat, a condition of vitality preservation. Simultaneously, probably, that improves the arrival of endorphins, which are the body's very own narcotic agony calming framework.

Moving out of Shutdown and Working with the Sympathetic Responses Underneath

As it were, individual movements from intense agony, to intense moving towards constant, and that is the thoughtful excitement/supporting example. At that point, after some time, it goes into the shutdown. So as to help individuals, when they've been in the shutdown, we need to figure out how to help get them a tad out of the shutdown and afterward utilize the thoughtful response under that. As Steve was stating, a great deal of that guidelines originates from that ventral vagal social commitment framework, by the advisor truly being available and having the option to direct them through those excitement sensations.

Researchers concur on the significant intercession of paunch breathing or stomach relaxing. A significant number of the extremely incredible afferents identified with relaxing for the ventral vagal system are really implanted in the stomach. The issue is, we can utilize a willful framework, which means control of the stomach and breathing, or possibly deliberate breathing, to drive the stomach down and to expand the span of exhalations just as to improve or build stomach relaxing. That, as it were, expands the ventral vagal stream. Once more, the fundamental hidden subject here is that the sympathetic in the dorsal vagal framework will work in a great homeostatic manner as long as the ventral vagus is truly working. Diminish has appeared in a solid manner that you can recover a portion of this control through a deliberate breathing system.

Since what that is doing is practically setting off the ventral vagus to empower the dorsal vagus and the sympathetic to return into a homeostatic circumstance. Propping, which obviously, is an increase in engine tone, is a thoughtful assembly and that has momentary impacts, as Levine proposes, "In case I'm holding my clench hands and planning, I am fundamentally saying to my ventral vagal framework, 'Leave since I'm in a guard mode.' Now, if this doesn't dispose of the agony, since I'm in a progressive framework, or I am a various leveled framework, I've just discarded, disposed of the ventral vagus as an alternative. On the off chance that this doesn't work, what does my sensory system do? It goes down to its most minimal level." We can't state that all the dorsal vagal reactions are negative in light of the fact that there is a level of absence of pain and now and again there is separation and no sentiment of agony. Yet, the expense of social collaboration is a cataclysmic cost to pay. When working with a customer, it's imperative to respect and regard the requirement for that specific guard framework and afterward step by step help the customer to move out of it to a less, more progressively contemporary framework, a present time and place framework.

Attention was payed to that a ton of advisors downgrade the freeze reaction and are practically phobic about it. They don't need the customer to be in a frozen state. It's critical to comprehend what sort of psycho-instruction we can give customers about how the freeze has been important to them.

Diminish includes that the freeze is a versatile reaction, implying that it has the versatile capacity and that is a piece of the psycho instructive part. At the point when individuals begin to comprehend that their body has responded, truly, in an anticipated and versatile way, it's not willful conduct. You can say: "Well mastered, I in the event that I would not like to close down; I shouldn't have closed down." But shut down is anything but an intentional framework. The body is getting things done outside the domains of mindfulness. Despite the fact that we don't know about the triggers that put us into these physiological states, the afferent input of our physiological moves positively is inside the domain of our mindfulness.

The issue is how would we name those physiological reactions? Do we reveal to ourselves that we accomplished something incorrectly or do we attempt to state, "Look, my body's accomplishing something? It might have been successful for an intense and versatile reaction, however clearly in the incessant one, the body should be corrected to state: 'Hello, it's sheltered, leave there.' Another significant factor is that when somebody leaves the shutdown, you ordinarily hear, "I didn't hurt that much previously." When the separation and the absence of pain break up, there's agony both physically and inwardly. As experts, we need to utilize instruction that fundamentally clarifies it that way. At that point, we must be available and accessible to help them at that point work through the torment. Nothing is settled - torment and injury issues don't resolve when the individual's in the shutdown - that will possibly occur on the off chance that they need to turn out enough to enable them to be vivaciously open.

Dwindle concurs that advisors are frequently awkward with the shutdown to arrange. This is likely because of a couple of variables. One is if specialists are scared of the freeze in themselves, of their own interior state. Another is that they basically don't have the foggiest idea of what to do. Most advisors are humane; they're giving it a second thought and, for the most part, well-tuned in for the customers. In the event that that is everything they do, in any case, it won't be adequate for somebody who's in a shutdown state.

The Importance of Breathing and Movement

There are various approaches to work with that, through the "voo" sound and immobilizing the jaw. For instance, the sort of breathing, that is discussed, is to utilize something like "Vooooooo." When the customer is approached to make the "voo" sound with you, you're associating the gut and afterward activating the jaw to help discharge the shutdown and freeze. Frequently in treatment, the customers are fundamentally drooped over like this. Regardless of whether the advisor says "Allows simply stroll around the room together", some of the time that is sufficient to deliver them out of their shutdown enough to begin reaching once more, it was looked at getting guidelines that should be amicable by moving among thoughtful and dorsal vagal and ventral vagal. To state it another way, we help customers to have the experience of being in the now.

Another measurement is included, which is working with facial muscles. This is a piece of what he calls the incorporated social commitment framework, which is giving enormous tangible criticism to the brain stem territory, directing the ventral vagus. It includes utilizing laryngeal, pharyngeal, trigeminal, and facial muscles in addition to tuning in. It's a coordinated framework.

Relaxing

Incredible specialist clarifies that is extremely great about breathing that we don't consider it when we do it. "We can think and do it another way, so it resembles a framework that we can actually venture into our body and change an unconstrained physiological framework. In the event that you watch customer's breath, or watch an on-edge individual, or a discouraged individual or an individual who is absolutely dissociative, you can really observe diverse breathing examples. A few scientists have really spent his life watching these kinds of things. We can look as an individual gets on edge, the breathing climbs their chest as they're truly getting shallow breaths, however, what happens is losing the chance of getting the critical impact of the stomach afferents going upwards to the ribs. All the more critically, the individual is lessening the span of the exhalation in the breath. It is during that exhalation that the ventral vagus can have a relieving impact.

At the point when analyst doing their breathing utilizing voo sounds, he is accentuating the breath out in light of the fact that else you would not have the sound; he's not sounding on the inward breath, he's sounding on the exhalation and he's empowering his customers and the advisors who utilize this system to broaden the span of their sounds. The expanded span of the exhalation implies from a polyvagal point of view, we broaden the effect of the ventral vagus."

Afferents

The contrast among afferents and Afferents by clarifying that the expression "efferent" implies that these are the nerves that are going from the mind, the brain stem for this situation, down to the viscera. "For instance, in the event that I willfully advise this hand to go into a clench hand, I'm doing that through Inference. Presently I'm shutting my eyes and I'm directing Beethoven's Fifth Symphony and afterward blast, 'If you don't mind, help me God,' I couldn't do that without afferents. Afferents are sending data from my muscles and my joints and furthermore from the viscera that educates me regarding my inward state. This can't be overstressed in sentiments of goodness and completeness – how significantly they are identified with our interior state. These receptors that are in the organs, which are in the muscles that are in the joints, are returning from the outskirts into the centrum, the mind, and the brain stem. This gives us information on who we are inside ourselves."

Some specialist includes that the afferents from the subdiaphragmatic region are once in a while perceived. "We know about it when it will, in general, be on the negative side. Subdiaphragmatically, when things are going extraordinary and the afferents and efferent are doing the suitable guideline, we're ignorant of it. Our mindfulness accompanies torment and inconvenience.

The part that I truly need to underscore is the place we have a brilliant jargon of outer sensation; we have an extremely constrained jargon for the viscera since we don't have the particularity of the instinctive receptors. It's not so much that we don't have every one of the words; we don't have all the attentive sentiments. At the point when we state 'I feel full in the wake of eating,' a portion of that isn't even an instinctive reaction. Some of it is really the stretch on the skin of our stomach area, which isn't originating from inside our guts; it's originating all things considered."

The principal year of Somatic Experiencing is finding out about those hundred, or thousands of various types of inside sensations and what they mean. We're figuring out how to explore them in the internal scene and obviously torment and injury and shut-down significantly moves you away from that procedure. It gives you this one experience of misery in the gut rather than the many subtlety sensation-based emotions that exude from a center instinctive feeling of ourselves.

Aggravation

Aggravation assumes a major job in torment. This area of our introduction thinks about how the autonomic sensory system directs agony and irritation. It begins by getting some information about the vagus nerve having receptors, some of which are influenced by cytokines, the resistant framework for incendiary action. At the point when a portion of the receptors activated by confined cytokines, discharge, this really illuminates the mind to discharge those equivalent sorts of synthetics midway. It's sort of a switchboard, so you have a receptor down beneath to get something and it sends the message "upstairs." It doesn't really go up the nerve in the feeling of the substance going up there. It's really a code.

When discussing irritation in the autonomic sensory system, the expression "ANS" might be excessively prohibitive. It was utilized the so called extended autonomic sensory system (see section 2). That term joins neuroendocrine and invulnerable and even adult individuals use as far as neuropeptides, similar to oxytocin and vasopressin. The explanation these structures are remembered for the extended ANS is that they're using comparative mind stem territories for guidelines. The apportioning of these controls, regardless of whether through psychoneural immunology or psychoendocrinology or psychophysiology demonstrate division with discrete ward factors, yet on the off chance that you take a gander at the guidelines frameworks, they're all covering.

The HPA (Hypothalamic Pituitary Adrenal Axis)

The piece of the mind that is a sort of driver of these autonomic and endocrine frameworks is the thing that has recently been known as the hypothalamic pituitary adrenal pivot (HPA). At the point when you have moved in autonomic action, you likewise get parallel moves in this hypothalamic-pituitary-adrenal hub (HPA), which influences not just irritation through the corticosteroid framework for instance, however practically the entirety of the inside metabolic and endocrinological exercises. It's extremely critical to comprehend this clinically. At the point when you work with a customer and you're working principally with their autonomic signs. At the point when they get guidelines there, all the time, individuals with immune system ailments or powerless insusceptible reactions will move. When we work with this focal pivot, a wide range of things can occur. W.R. Hess, who won the Nobel Prize in 1949, indicated that the nerve center really influences for all intents and purposes all aspects of the mind and the sensory system in the body. It is surprising that individuals don't speak much about that any longer.

Hess won the Nobel Prize in 1949 for his work on the focal guideline of the viscera. In the main passage of his discourse, he depicts how everything is interrelated to everything else in the body. He is stating that the connection among the parts is substantially more than the entirety of the little segments. Diminish and I am enormous adherents to his work.

The Dorsal Vagal and Nociception as a Cause of Pain

There's a great deal of installed look into drifting around in neurophysiology on the connection between the afferents of the dorsal vagus and nociception (the encoding and preparing of destructive boosts in the sensory system, and in this way the body's capacity to detect potential damage). Something revealed is that the tactile piece of the vagus associates with a spinal pathway that is engaged with nociception. That gets fascinating regarding develops or ideas like fibromyalgia, which will, in general, be connected particularly with individuals who have encountered significant shutdown and are truly coasting between a dorsal state and a thoughtful state. They're closing down. In the event that you just followed their colon, you'd presumably observe a similar wonder. It could be said going among obstruction and looseness of the bowels; you'd locate a similar representation at a lower level. What you need to comprehend is that two or three things get truly activated because of the changing in the afferent guideline of the autonomic sensory system while in a dorsal vagal state.

That implies that the framework that manages circulatory strain guidelines, the baroreceptors, gets disturbed. Individuals frequently get dazed and drop. They become "vasovagal thoughtful," they fall, and this is because of vagal afferents. It's a framework that isn't connected, so just a piece of it is working. Individuals regularly displaying these issues may have hypotension or hypertension. It's the circulatory strain guideline. Hess found the connection between ceaseless weakness disorder and pulse guideline issues that they are a piece of a similar system.

We may have three disorders connected together as far as symptomatology. One is the interminable weakness which will be an indication of numerous individuals who have an injury or who have encountered drawn-out periods in dorsal vagal states. The second is pulse guideline, not hypertension, yet actually getting dazed when holding up. This isn't the sort of unsteadiness where things are turning, however, where the individual truly begins hitting the ground. The third connection is fibromyalgia. These are no different systems - fibromyalgia, incessant weakness, and pulse guideline - that have gone hypotensive. This is all piece of the dorsal vagus framework, in the sense, being the final retreat and being utilized in a guarded mode.

These three troubles are aspects of a similar disorder. These side effects were deconstructed, so we can discuss every one of these indications and how they would depict fibromyalgia, circulatory strain guideline, and ceaseless exhaustion. In the event that the individual is spending a lot of their neuro-guideline time in a dorsal vagal express that isn't secured with the highlights of wellbeing, we can't immobilize unafraid.

Dread and Depression, Polyvagal Science, and Pain

Extraordinary analyst accentuates dread and wretchedness as far as polyvagal science and torment. Frequently when the torment gets interminable, the adjustment to allostatic load (the mileage on the body because of incessant pressure) is to move towards shutdown. This happens in light of the fact that there is dread related to the heap and sorrow that will, in general, fortify itself. Ordinarily, in creatures that are undermined, or under life risk won't move. They give off an impression of being dead. Much the same as a gazelle that will be brought somewhere near a cheetah. There's no development; however, then minutes after the fact, the creature just bounces up and goes off on its way. Since those states are ordinarily time-restricted. Be that as it may, when you bring dread into the stability circuit, it keeps up idleness or freeze; however, it keeps up it powerfully.

How about we take a guinea pig for a model, at the point when you take the guinea pig and grasp it, it gets stable. At that point in almost no time, seconds to minutes, it springs up and goes off. Be that as it may, on the off chance that you scare it each time it goes in, it remains longer. What could be five minutes or seven seconds, with the dread included, can for all intents and purposes keep it uncertainly. Subside did an analysis like that in Brazil and had the creature remain in that state for 24 hours. In some cases, creatures will really bite the dust. Dangers and Benefits in Coming Out of Immobility

At the point when an individual starts to leave fixed status, clinically, there's a surge of hyper excitement. Porges was discussing the thoughtful and dorsal vagal framework being in this sort of flip-flop. What you need to do is help the individual contain the thoughtful framework, by keeping them connected socially in the present time and place. At that point, there is a guideline and the stationary individual can leave the fixed status, out of the dorsal vagal shutdown, in light of the fact that they're not reactivating themselves. On the off chance that the agony turns out to be increasingly intense, you need to state: "OK".

In the event that that agony turns out to be progressively intense and you simply start to see that somewhat more, you notice if it's proceeding to increment if it's beginning to diminish or in the event that it continues as before or on the off chance that it changes to something different". With this sort of greeting, customers get the feeling that time moves along and blast, before they know it, they've left from the stability state.

It has been clarified that a few warm-blooded animals, through phylogenetic advancement, can go all through polyvagal responses as versatile capacities. Little rodents additionally do this: in any case, even in going into the dorsal vagal reaction for a little rat, there's a danger of dropping dead. The equivalent is valid with the guinea pig; there is an opportunity simply dropping dead from the immobilization reaction. This probability will, in general, happen with mice and other little rodents. What gives off an impression of being versatile can likewise be deadly; as warm-blooded creatures, we need bunches of oxygen, and when we go into shutdown states, we're not supporting our life needs just as our body needs.

Another part to recall is the thought of when the creatures leave dorsal vagal states, they shut down and they get profoundly immobilized. There is likewise a feeling of an exceptionally prepared state for some versatile reasons, and one is simply to getaway. They are attempting to recover the blood into their muscles, over into their bodies with the goal that they presently have the suitable metabolic assets to move the muscles. You have these jerks and different things that are happening as you refuel the body. At that point, the guideline begins happening. For whatever length of time that people who have recently experienced closed down are assembled, which implies that they are in a condition of frenzy or turmoil, they won't shut down. You need to consider these to be as having versatile highlights. They are not so many highlights of good social communication, yet they keep them out of closing down. Our sensory system has advanced, perfectly and articulately to move among assembly and social collaboration. That characterizes how warm-blooded creatures work and develop and endure, on the grounds that they needed to recognize quickly, who was protected and who was undependable.

The Dorsal Vagus, Goodness, and Help with Pain

Dwindle follows up prior exchange to speak all the more explicitly about the way that numerous advisors, when they find out about the dorsal vagal framework, and its focal job in injury and in ceaseless torment, will consider it to be the adversary. It's practically similar to "well, on the off chance that we could remove it, is there any valid reason why you wouldn't simply remove it?" Why not cut out those afferent and efferent associations? The explanation is that the dorsal vagal framework in vertebrates or people is extremely integral to essential sentiments of goodness and furthermore underpins sentiments of association through the ventral vagal framework. At the point when you feel warm and upbeat, you can get an aching "God; it'd be superb in the event that we could return to our strolls on the seashore, etc." Feelings of joy and those emotions, they originate from the gut. They originate from the stomach and they originate from the heart. What we're discussing is a framework that is so essential for our very own working, yet can so promptly get maladaptive and specialists need to comprehend and hold together the two sides of this.

"Wouldn't we be able to remove it? Wouldn't we be able to discourage it?" They are feeling the loss of the entire comprehension of what's happening and that is the reason if that framework is utilized as a cautious framework, it can't be a framework that supports our homeostatic needs. The equivalent is valid for the sympathetic. To conceptualize this present, a term wasn't preferred much called "Autonomic Balance." Autonomic Balance alluded to the way that as it were you have enough sympathetic and enough parasympathetic. Rather Porges stresses that "On the off chance that the ventral vagal circuit is truly working great, at that point sub diaphragmatically you have [organically] autonomic harmony between the sympathetic and the dorsal vagus." This is the sort of equalization you need to have and this advances nice sentiments. He notes that there was an inclination of prosperity and how that climbs the afferent vagus from the gut and truly rules our capacity to get to various regions of our mind. We should not overlook this enormous progression of tangible data that is basically originating from underneath the stomach that is really changing the availability to different pieces of our brain. It's a screen. The main problem is the capacity to keep the thoughtful and dorsal frameworks out of guarded jobs. They will be utilized for resistance at different occasions just as for their versatile capacities and on the off chance that they're intense, the parity presumably will be okay, particularly the sympathetic. On the off chance that it's drawn out, and if the sympathetic doesn't work to get us out of threat, we get into this dorsal resistance framework. That is truly where we get into issues.

Our life structures naturally close things down. In case we're not in a cautious mode, the agony isn't brought about by something natural. That all the time is the point at which you can have the individual interface with some instinctive sentiments of goodness, of alright ness of prosperity, to move to and fro between those sensations and the territory of the body where the torment is. "Ok, so you feel that torment in your shoulder, in your correct shoulder, yet then you additionally feel that sentiment of warmth and extension in your paunch. On the off chance that you let yourself move between these two sensations, notice what occurs, what changes, and afterward, what occurs straightaway?" You can enroll in those nice sentiments. Be that as it may, once more, if the body is truly in extreme agony and it gets incessant, the customer is going to be in a shutdown state. A great many people think about whether there's a science behind this in light of the fact that there are many investigations that view the incitement of vagal afferents as mediators or modulators of physical torment. Levine is proposing that we can move our instinctive sentiments to manage the torment, how about we take an inclination that includes a subdiaphragmatic gut reaction that changes the afferent stream, changing our real state to make it simpler to manage the agony. Similarly, as though we would get the medical procedure (I'm sharing my very own arrangement of encounters here) in a confiding in the way, our tissue is extremely substantially more malleable. We won't scar to such an extent and we'll mend sooner. The issue is trusting and feeling great, having nice sentiments. Utilizing those mental develops in explicit physiological states, distinctive tactile afferents are regulating our torment receptors and balancing the receptors of safeguard on the tissue level. We have a barrier on various levels. The body responds progressively from, it could be said, social correspondence of parts of the body, much the same as the polyvagal theory. At that point, it goes down as it ensures its components and afterward, at long last, it implodes. It goes into a real existence danger mode and implodes.

According to, Bob Naviaux, who is a doctor who runs the metabolic mitochondrial center at U.C. San Diego, microbes pursue the Polyvagal Theory. He says, "When things are great and when it's everything clear" is the representation he employs. "They converse with one another, they're intuitive. They are socially captivating." Now present a risk to the framework and it essentially makes its own protections. At that point, you can close them down, they implode and they cease to exist. The allegory of security socialization is as it were a representation of the human body at all levels.

This is a piece of the investigations of the small scale bile. This gets us back to the gut and the afferents. On the off chance that you signal that the stomach related framework will close down, creatures start dropping their pulses, and go into a shutdown response – this occurs with mice. The sign of the gut is currently passed on up the vagus to the brain stem saying: "Hello, this is awful!" Now we're examining techniques for turning around the intense injury, by essentially sending a sign up the gut saying: "Hello, everything's unmistakable." There are pharmaceutical or pharmacological strategies for sending an "all reasonable" reaction through the gut, through the receptors of the gut.

We're going to truly do an examination that applies an intense injury to the prairie vole, through limitation and predator. We essentially put him in a limitation, which is awful enough. At that point, we put his characteristic predator, a ferret, before them. A portion of their basal pulses are 400; some of them simply get tachycardia. They go up to 600. Be that as it may, others go down to 150 beats for each moment, some shutdown and seem as though they're dead. Be that as it may, there is likewise species decent variety.

It might be said, this makes the adaptively of animal types to endure. The issue of what we need to consider is at one time that vole has gone into shutdown, what befalls their social conduct, their parenting conduct? We need to invert it by sending a gut reaction up to the brain, "State, hello, your gut's everything great." Will that be adequate to turn them around?

There is a medication that animates the typical motioning of the gut that all is well, yet that is not the sole arrangement since it's a multifaceted issue as injury seems to be. He's likewise utilizing highlights of medications that he has created with acoustic incitement offering prompts to the vole in light of the fact that the voles are vocal and they vocalize as their very own sign autonomic state. On the off chance that they're worried, the prosodic element of the vole vocalization exhibits that.

Functional Ways of Shifting Out of the Freeze

Diminish has discovered that occasionally it's conceivable to do various things with activating. He has a gadget that resembles a little trampoline, yet it's totally unique. It doesn't utilize any springs and it has flexible bungee ropes. Presently when somebody remains on this, one arrives at a spot where he/she starts to, as it were, have cooperation with the trampoline. It feels like that the trampoline needs to move you a smidgen, to ricochet you a little minuscule piece and as you feel that skipping, you're getting new proprioceptive data, assembling data from the joints, from the muscles. Diminish works with individuals in serious shutdown, and accepts that doing verbal treatment could go on until the following century! Simply getting these little developments on this trampoline takes them out enough so they're available to versatility and you can work with them. It's great to recall that there are non-verbal and development situated methods for doing this.Porges' viewpoint is consistently to deconstruct what is by all accounts attempting to give it a physiological approval. Where instincts appear to be truly on target, would we be able to give a motivation behind why? There are two things. One is shaking. Many people who have these encounters will regularly do things like this, and they need to comprehend that they are animating vagal afferents and attempting to direct circulatory strain through the development of their body in space. It's not simply body and space. They are really animating the carotid baroreceptors. It's mitigating for individuals to shake. We need to consider it to be a neural exercise, as an endeavor to restore a framework that has been down controlled.

Another way brings up the entire issue of the pelvic floor. A great deal of people who have injury encounters understands that a large number of these injury encounters will be precisely related, particularly stomach medical procedure or sub-stomach medical procedure. The pelvic floor is going to, it might be said, quit working. We need to comprehend that the pelvic floor is, as a similitude, a stomach. Similarly, as our stomach is to our lungs, the pelvic floor is to our bladder and colon.

It makes a negative weight. The pelvic floor contracts, so everybody who has had pelvic floor issues is told, "Do Kegel works out." But Kegel practices are sphincter muscles. The pelvic floor isn't a sphincter muscle, it has sphincter muscles crossing it. How would you get the pelvic floor to change and work? You do that through moving parity or parity challengers. This resembles the methodology with the trampoline. We may likewise utilize the BOSU, which is half of an activity ball. Subside concurs that simply sitting on a gymnastic ball and making little developments, and afterward finding support to discover the sentiment of giving up the pelvic floor into the ball can truly move things. On the off chance that the individual enables the ball to help the pelvic stomach, the stomach just unwinds into the ball. You see this regularly with sexual injury, stomach medical procedures, etc. Porges saw that Levine shut his eyes while depicting this procedure. His eyes began to hang and close. That helped to remember the way that he had a medical procedure and I didn't care for what they instructed him to do, to manage the pelvic floor issues, so he made his very own model. He likewise understood that in the event that he shut his eyes, it was increasingly troublesome and testing, and it was working better since he was not utilizing the obvious prompts. It's ideal to work with customers with their eyes open and something to clutch. It makes a connectedness on the off chance that you are with someone else. You can even give them your arm to clutch with the goal that when they leave shut down, there you are.

Substantial Resources of the Dorsal Vagal

From Porges' perspective, it's a troublesome inquiry. It could be said, it's our center or our base of being alive and the issue is that when we attempt to utilize it as an asset, it's practically similar to utilizing it as a resistance. Rather, we need to sustain it. At the point when we support it, it serves us and this is the place the afferents are returning saying: "all unmistakable". The "every single clear" afferent are similar afferents that help our capacity to draw in others and our capacity to get to different territories of the mind that are both social and innovative. On the off chance that the sign from the dorsal vagus is, "I'm in a difficult situation," it will down direct everything else. It's an emotionally supportive network, an asset framework, whereby giving; we get, instead of a feeling of abuse from it.

The Dorsal Vagal Shutdown

The last subject for this discourse is, what counsel would you provide for specialists who are working with customers with ceaseless serious agony that gives off an impression of being identified with the dorsal vagal shutdown protective reaction? Where might you propose they start? The dorsal-vagal shutdown reaction is looking down, looking anyplace else. You can simply tell they are going into a freeze since they are unbending and very de-centered, we as a whole realize what it resembles. Dwindle proposes saying: "It appears as though it's extremely hard for you to talk at this moment, if that is valid, what about both of us simply stroll around the room a bit." When I lived in Colorado full time, and on the waterway, I would take customers out into the yard on the property and stroll around the stream. You could simply observe things move. Development additionally brings out interest. In any case, regardless of whether they can get inquisitive about the shutdown at that point, you've enrolled them as a partner. They watch themselves as a partner. On the off chance that somebody is in a shutdown, it's not simply freezing. It's more identified with the thoughtful despite the fact that it has segments of both.

I think the basic thing here is that when the individual is in the breakdown when you can't utilize your intelligence to get the individual to move, or inhale, and commonly when an individual has been tremendously damaged, particularly explicitly, to make a voo sound toward the start would be excessive. Strolling around the room is probably going to be alright, perhaps in any event, hopping a smidgen on that trampoline that I talked about. Once more, you can be there and hold their hand while they're doing it and afterward, when they show fervor, state "Amazing, that is awesome, appears as though you are truly feeling more vitality." You have to reach. On the off chance that its stresses they have, they need to discuss their stresses. On the off chance that its agony and what impact it has on their life, at that point let them talk about that for some time and afterward get the chance to "Alright, so now we should start to take care of that; would you say you are energetic about me?"

For whatever length of time that you make them move in a manner that isn't a battle flight development, they are going to avoid profound separation or closing down in light of the fact that, as we've stated, there's a chain of command in physiological states and on the off chance that you move you can't close down. On the off chance that you can move now in a socially strong condition, you're presently playing out a sort of neural exercise and one where the individual is picking up the capacity to move more with regards to play than they were in battle or flight.

For whatever length of time that you can remain in a moving state, without going into fight/flight, at that point, there is the chance of enrolling the social commitment frameworks and the ventral vagus since that is the gateway we have. We don't have a decent entryway of going straightforwardly out of the dorsal vagus. What we have is a gateway that in case we're gently prepared, we can push individuals or trigger individuals into increasingly social commitment.

Attention was called to that without the social vagal framework being on the web somehow or another, at any rate in connection to you as an expert, at that point the customer will most likely be unable to move out of the dorsal vagal reaction, particularly since there is no immediate entry to come legitimately out of shutdown and stability guards. The polyvagal theory advises us that the other point that is extremely basic is that when individuals are incautious states, they're going to peruse impartial signs in your face and in your conduct as negative. You must be cautious about losing contact, not being available and dismissing, doing trifling things that typically would not make any difference. Customers may, as it were, exaggerate and turn out to be exceptionally responsive and afterward vanish again on the mental level.

Dwindle makes reference to that everything is somewhat one-sided towards bogus positives. That is the reason seen danger is an endurance reaction. You generally have your discernment. I was simply expounding on this, on the memory book. Laura and I were altering this segment of the book and we took a break, strolling around. We were in Zurich, one of the most delightful of parks. We're strolling and clasping hands, and unexpectedly, we're ready to readiness. We're loathing each other's organization, No all the more clasping hands and strolling, presently, the two of us are looking and filtering – it's just as there is some frightful danger. We saw around 20 bamboo branches; the children are waving them around and not complying with the ordinary Swiss standards.Presently recall that we feel that Zurich is the most secure spot on the planet. A recreation center like this is presumably about the most secure park in the most secure spot in the whole world. In any case, we are customized to anticipate the most noticeably terrible. We are modified to anticipate dangers. When we understood what it was, we chuckled and returned along our way. In any case, on the off chance that you've been undermined and harmed by an individual, any small seemingly insignificant detail about their face that reminds you even remotely is going to trigger them. You can't stay away from it totally, so you may, in some cases, ask, "It appears as though something I said or didn't state, appeared to disrupt the general flow, or influence you?" Again, you're helping them articulate a portion of this, which likewise is a method for bringing the frontal brain on the web and the social commitment framework on the web.

Another piece of experience is the acoustic condition. Individuals tend not to stress that. At the point when you're in a hyper-careful express, your hearing gets one-sided towards low recurrence sounds or shrill ones. It loses its keenness in the scope of prosodic highlights of a human voice. We lose incomprehension, or we hose our capacity to comprehend others' effects around us on the grounds that the low frequencies are triggers of predators. The high frequencies are triggers of somebody in torment, when those bamboo grasses, which weren't grass however 20 feet high – when they were moving, there was most likely a low recurrence murmur that was originating from them. That, to all warm-blooded animals, is predatorial. The body is modified to respond naturally to predators.

This part has exhibited a powerful discourse of the dorsal vagal segment of the polyvagal framework and its unpredictable collaborations with the ventral vagal social commitment framework and with the thoughtful/adrenal battle flight arrangement of guard and guideline.

One of the most significant rules that were underlined on numerous occasions in various manners is the significance of acquiring security through ventral vagal social commitment. In the treatment of injury and agony, this must be practiced by guiding the mending relationship through what was named "natural discourteousness" as meaningful gestures are misconstrued, acoustical sounds are seen as hazardous and predatorial, and the two individuals from the relationship are activated to pull back Despite the fact that this is incredibly testing work, there is a lot of expectation in the procedures offered here. The endowment of basic nearness can support resistance and shutdown move to the association and recuperate. Stomach breathing and "voo" sounding expand the exhalation and the relieving sentiment of ventral vagal commitment. Basic development, like strolling around the workplace can help customers who have incredible trouble with social commitment through "eye to eye" connection and other associations. We can help thoughtful regulation by training jargon to our customers so they can remain associated with their very own body understanding and to us. Empowering development on an activity ball or extraordinary trampoline that is protected and expands social commitment is enormously mending. Delicate shaking developments can comparably be a protected and agreeable approach to enter the ventral vagal framework while starting to move out of shutdown. At last, keeping an eye on the acoustic condition and improving the prosodic characteristics of the advisor's voice can likewise extend the ventral vagal commitment, so each of the three branches helps move the living being into homeostasis and completeness.

CHAPTER NINE: CLINICAL APPLICATIONS OF THE POLYVAGAL THEORY

Creative clinicians share their encounters coordinating Polyvagal Theory into their treatment models. Clinicians who have committed their work to bring the advantages of the Polyvagal Theory to a scope of customers have met up to present Polyvagal Theory in an innovative and individual manner. Sections on a scope of points from merciful medicinal consideration to advanced restorative connections to clinician's encounters as Parents remove from the theory the amazing impact and significance of cases and sentiments of security in the clinical setting.

Also, there are sections which: expand on the guideline of wellbeing in clinical practice with kids with misuse narratives clarify the helpful outcomes of development, cadence, and move in advancing social connectedness and versatility in injury survivors clarifies how Polyvagal Theory can be utilized to understand the neurophysiological procedures in different treatments talk about dissociative procedures and medications intended to encounter real sentiments of security and trust inspect dread of flying and how utilizing positive recollections as a functioning "base up" neuropeptide procedure may successfully down-control guard shed light on the ineffectively comprehended understanding of misery Through the bits of knowledge of creative and considerate clinicians, whose treatment models are Polyvagal educated, this book gives an available method to clinicians to grasp this noteworthy theory in their very own work.

Clinicians who have committed their work to bring the advantages of the Polyvagal Theory to a scope of customers have met up to present Polyvagal Theory in an inventive and individual way. Chapters on a scope of points from humane medicinal consideration to advanced remedial connections to clinician's encounters as Parents remove from the theory the amazing impact and significance of cases and sentiments of wellbeing in the clinical setting. Additionally, there are parts which: elaborate on the standard of security in clinical practice with youngsters with misuse histories explain the therapeutic outcomes of development, cadence, and move in advancing social connectedness and strength in injury survivors explains how Polyvagal Theory can be utilized to understand the neurophysiological procedures in different therapies discuss dissociative procedures and medications intended to encounter substantial sentiments of security and trust examine dread of flying and how utilizing positive recollections as a functioning "base up" neuropeptide procedure may successfully down-control defense shed light on the ineffectively comprehended understanding of grief through the bits of knowledge of creative and big-hearted clinicians.

Adult Attachment

The Adult Attachment Interview (AAI) is both a backbone of connection look into and a ground-breaking clinical instrument. This extraordinary book gives an intensive prologue to the AAI and its utilization as a subordinate to a scope of remedial methodologies, including cognitive-conductal treatment, psychoanalytic psycho-treatment, parent-baby psycho-treatment, home visiting programs, and strong work with regards to child care and selection.

Driving specialists give definite portrayals of clinical strategies and procedures, showed with striking case material. Grounded in inquiring about, the volume features how utilizing the AAI can improve evaluation and finding, fortify the remedial partnership, and encourage objective setting, treatment arranging, and progress checking.

Reframe Your Thinking Around Autism

The Polyvagal Theory proposes chemical imbalance is an educated reaction by the body - a consequence of the kid being in a drawn-out condition of 'battle or flight' while their sensory system is as yet creating. This section clarifies the theory in basic terms and consolidates ongoing advancements in mind versatility explore (the limit of the brain to change all through life) to give Parents and experts the devices to reinforce the kid's brain-body association and reduce the social and passionate effect of chemical imbalance.

An existence without outrage is feasible - in the event that you comprehend The Anger Fallacy. Outrage is all over - behind everything from street fierceness to wrap rage, aggressive conduct at home to universal clashes. Individuals stick to their annoyance, as an apparatus of impact and a driver of vengeance. In any case, is outrage actually ever helpful? Also, would we be able to figure out how to beat it? In this engaging and momentous book, two of Australia's driving clinical therapists adopt an extreme strategy to outrage the executives, detonating the nonsensical convictions that fuel this harmful and misjudged feeling.

Through various models from mainstream society and the counseling room, and with a sizable portion of cleverness, the creators tell the best way to battle outrage by subbing sympathy and comprehension for honorable irate decisions.

CHAPTER TEN:
YOGA TREATMENT AND THE POLYVAGAL THEORY

Yoga treatment is a recently developing, automatic correlative and integrative human services (CIH) practice. It is developing in its professionalization, acknowledgment & use with a showed responsibility to setting practice principles, instructive & accreditation norms, and elevating exploration to help its viability for different populaces and conditions.

In any case, heterogeneity of training, poor detailing principles, and absence of an extensively acknowledged comprehension of the neurophysiological systems associated with yoga treatment restrain the organizing of testable speculations and clinical applications.

Currently proposed structures of yoga-put together practices center with respect to the combination of base up neurophysiological and top-down neurocognitive components. What's more, it has been suggested that phenomenology and first individual moral request can give a focal point through which yoga treatment is seen as a procedure that contributes towards eudaimonic prosperity in the experience of torment, sickness or incapacity. In this article, we expand on these systems and propose a model of yoga treatment that merges with Polyvagal Theory (PVT).

PVT joins the development of the autonomic sensory system to the rise of prosocial practices and sets that the neural stages supporting social conduct are engaged with looking after wellbeing, development and reclamation. This logical model, which associates neurophysiological examples of autonomic guidelines and articulation of enthusiastic and social conduct, is progressively used as a system for understanding human conduct, stress and disease.

In particular, we portray how PVT can be conceptualized as a neurophysiological partner to the yogic ideal of the gunas, or characteristics of nature. Like the neural stages portrayed in PVT, the gunas give the establishment from which conduct, passionate and physical traits rise. We depict how these two distinct yet closely resembling structures - one situated in neurophysiology and the other in an old intelligence convention - feature yoga treatment's advancement of physical, mental and social prosperity for self-guideline and strength. This parallel between the neural foundation of PVT and the gunas of yoga is instrumental in making a translational structure for yoga treatment to line up with its philosophical establishments. Thusly, yoga treatment can work as a particular practice instead of fitting into an outside model for its usage in inquires about and clinical settings.

Mind-body treatments, including yoga treatment, are proposed to profit wellbeing and prosperity through reconciliation of top-down and base up forms encouraging bidirectional correspondence between the brain and body. Top-down procedures, for example, the guideline of consideration and setting of expectation, have been appeared to diminish mental worry just as the hypothalamic-pituitary pivot (HPA) and thoughtful sensory system (SNS) movement, and thusly balance insusceptible capacity and irritation. Base up forms, advanced by breathing procedures and development rehearses, have been appeared to impact the musculoskeletal, cardiovascular and sensory system work and furthermore influence HPA and SNS movement with attending changes in resistant capacity and passionate prosperity.

The top-down and base up forms utilized at the top of the priority list body treatments may control autonomic, neuroendocrine, enthusiastic and conduct actuation and bolster a person's reaction to challenges. Self-guideline, a cognizant capacity to keep up the security of the framework by overseeing or modifying reactions to risk or misfortune, may diminish side effects of differing conditions, for example, peevish inside disorder, neurodegenerative conditions, interminable agony, wretchedness and PTSD through the moderation of allostatic load with a going with the move-in autonomic state have proposed such a model of top-down and base up self-administrative components of yoga for mental wellbeing.

Versatility may give another advantage of mind-body treatments as it incorporates the capacity of a person to "ricochet back" and adjust in light of affliction as well as unpleasant conditions in an opportune manner to such an extent that psychophysiological assets are rationed. High strength is related to faster cardiovascular recuperation following abstract passionate encounters, less saw pressure, more noteworthy recuperation from ailment or injury and better administration of dementia and incessant agony. Traded off versatility is connected to dysregulation of the autonomic sensory system through proportions of vagal guidelines (respiratory sinus arrhythmia. Yoga is related to both improvement in proportions of mental strength and improved vagal guidelines.

This article investigates the mix of top-down and base up forms for self-guideline and versatility through both Polyvagal Theory and yoga treatment. PVT will be portrayed in connection to contemporary understandings of interoception just as the bioconductal theory of the "preliminary set", which will be characterized later. This will help to spread out an incorporated framework from which mind-body treatments encourage the development of physiological, enthusiastic and social qualities for the advancement of self-guideline and strength.

We will look at the union of the neural stages, depicted in PVT, with the three Gunas, a fundamental idea of yogic way of thinking that portrays the characteristics of material nature. Both PVT and yoga give structures to seeing how basic neural stages (PVT) and gunas (yoga) interface the development and availability between physiological, mental and conduct characteristics. By influencing the neural stage, or guna transcendence, just as one's relationship to the ceaseless moving of these neural stages, or gunas, the individual learns aptitudes for self-guideline and strength. In addition, these structures share qualities that parallel each other where the neural stage mirrors the guna power and the guna prevalence mirrors the neural stage. PVT, and other rising hypotheses, for example, neurovisceral combination, help explain associations between the frameworks of the body, the brain, and the procedures of the mind offering expanded understanding into complex examples of incorporated top-down and base up forms that are natural to mind-body treatments. PVT portrays three particular neural stages in light of apparent hazard (i.e., wellbeing, peril, and life-risk) in the condition that works in a phylogenetically decided chain of command steady with the Jacksonian guideline of disintegration. PVT acquaints the idea of neuroception with depicting the subliminal recognition of wellbeing or peril in nature through base up forms including vagal afferents, tangible info identified with outside difficulties, and endocrine components that recognize and assess ecological hazard before the cognizant elaboration by higher mind focuses.

The three polyvagal neural stages, as portrayed underneath, are connected to the practices of social correspondence, guarded procedure of activation and protective immobilization:

The ventral vagal complex (VVC) gives the neural structures that intervene in the "social commitment framework". At the point when wellbeing is recognized in the interior and outside condition, the VVC gives a neural stage to help prosocial conduct and social association by connecting the neural guideline of instinctive states supporting homeostasis and reclamation to facial expressivity and the open and expressive areas of correspondence (e.g., prosodic vocalizations and upgraded capacity to tune in to voice). The engine segment of the VVC, which starts in the core ambiguous (NA) manages and organizes the muscles of the face and head with the bronchi and heart. These associations help arrange the individual towards human association and commitment in prosocial connections and give increasingly adaptable and versatile reactions to ecological difficulties including social communications

The SNS is oftentimes connected with battle/flight practices. Battle/flight practices require initiation of the SNS and are the underlying and essential guard procedures enlisted by warm-blooded creatures. This safeguard technique requires expanded metabolic yield to help activation practices. Inside PVT, the enlistment of SNS in guard pursues the Jacksonian guideline of disintegration and mirrors the versatile responses of a phylogenetically requested reaction progressively in which the VVC has neglected to alleviate risk. At the point when the SNS circuit is selected, there are monstrous physiological changes remembering an expansion for muscle tone, shunting of blood from the fringe, restraint of gastrointestinal capacity, an enlargement of the bronchi, increments in pulse and respiratory rate, and arrival of catecholamines.

This assembly of physiological assets makes way for reacting to genuine or accepted peril in the earth and towards the ultimate objectives of security and endurance. At the point when the SNS turns into the predominant neural stage, the VVC impact might be repressed for activating assets for a quick activity. Though prosocial practices and social associations are related to the VVC, the SNS is related to practices and feelings, for example, dread or outrage that help to arrange to the earth for security or wellbeing.

The dorsal vagal complex (DVC) emerges from the dorsal core of the vagus (DNX) and gives the essential vagal engine filaments to organs situated beneath the stomach. This circuit is intended to adaptably react to massive peril or dread and is the crudest (i.e., developmentally most established) reaction to stretch. Initiation of the DVC in resistance brings about an uninvolved reaction portrayed by diminished muscle tone, and emotional decrease of heart yield to save metabolic assets, modification in gut and bladder work by means of reflexive poop and pee to lessen metabolic requests required by processing.

PVT sets that through these neural stages, specific physiological states, mental traits, and social procedures are associated, develop, and are made open to the person. The physiological state built up by these neural stages in light of risk or security (as decided through the coordinated procedures of neuroception) takes into consideration or limits the scope of passionate and social attributes that are open to the person

A center part of PVT is those examples of physiological state, feeling and conduct are specific to each neural stage (for a point by point audit of the neurophysiological, neuroanatomical, and developmental natural bases of

PVT. For instance, the neural foundation of the VVC is proposed to associate instinctive homeostasis with passionate qualities and prosocial practices that are contradictory with the neurophysiological states, enthusiastic attributes or social practices that show in the neural foundation of protective procedures found in SNS or DVC initiation. At the point when the VVC is predominant, the vagal brake is executed and pro-social practices and enthusiastic states, for example, association and love can possibly develop.

At the point when the SNS is the essential guarded system, the NA kills the inhibitory activity of the ventral vagal pathway to the heart to empower thoughtful enactment and social and passionate procedures of assembly are bolstered. On the off chance that the DVC idleness reaction is the cautious system, the dorsal engine core is initiated as a defensive component from agony or potential demise and dynamic reaction methodologies are not accessible. It is imperative to take note of the VVC has different qualities that empower mixed states with the SNS (e.g., play) or with the DVC (e.g., closeness). Be that as it may, in these instances of mixed states, the VVC remains effectively available and practically contains the subordinate circuits. At the point when the VVC is practically pulled back, it advances the availability of the SNS as a guard battle/flight framework. So also, the SNS practically restrains access to the DVC immobilization shutdown reaction. In this way, the significant shutdown response that may prompt demise turns out to be neurophysiologically available just when the SNS is reflexively repressed.

Vagal Activity, Interoception, Regulation, and Resilience

Vagal movement, by means of ventral vagal pathways, is recommended to be intelligent of guideline and versatility of the framework where high heart vagal tone associated with increasingly versatile top-down and base up procedures, for example, consideration guideline, full of feeling preparing and adaptability of physiological frameworks to adjust and react to the earth. Vagal control has additionally been appeared to relate with differential actuation in mind locales that manage reactions to risk evaluation, interoception, feeling guideline, and the advancement of more noteworthy adaptability in light of challenge. On the other hand, the low vagal guideline has been related with maladaptive base up and top-down handling bringing about poor self-guideline, less social adaptability, discouragement, summed up uneasiness issue, and antagonistic wellbeing results remembering expanded mortality for conditions, for example, lupus, rheumatoid joint pain, and injury.

The vagus nerve is involved 80% afferent filaments and fills in as a significant conductor for interoceptive correspondence about the condition of the viscera and inside milieu to brain structures. Interoception has been investigated as basic to the connecting of top-down and base up preparing and in the examination of the connections between sensations, feelings, sentiments and sympathovagal. Backing has been found for the joining of interoceptive info, feeling and a guideline of sympathovagal balance in the separate and cingulate cortices, encouraging a bound together reaction of the person to body, mind or natural (BME) wonders.

Self-guideline is proposed to be subject to the precision with which we decipher and react to interoceptive data, with more prominent exactness prompting upgraded versatility and self-guideline. Thusly, interoception is viewed as significant in torment, habit, enthusiastic guideline, and solid versatile practices, including social commitment. Furthermore, interoception has been proposed as key to versatility as the precise preparation of interior substantial states advances a brisk rebuilding of homeostatic parity.

It has been suggested that mind-body treatments are a successful device for the guideline of vagal capacity, with resulting encouraging of versatile capacities including the alleviation of unfavorable impacts related with social difficulty, the decrease of allostatic load, and the assistance of self-administrative abilities and strength of the ANS crosswise over different patient populaces and conditions.

Polyvagal Theory & Mind-Body Therapies for Regulation & Resilience

Mind-body treatments underscore the development of physical mindfulness, including both interoception and proprioception, joined with the care based characteristics of non-judgment, non-reactivity, interest, or acknowledgment so as to take part in a procedure of re-evaluation of improvements. While being urged to develop familiarity with BME wonders and boosts, the individual is bolstered in a procedure of re-elucidation or re-direction to such improvements, so understanding may happen and flexibility, guideline, and versatility might be cultivated.

This ability to change the relationship and response to BME wonders is believed to be fundamental for self-guideline and prosperity. It has been indicated that patients using mind-body treatments for recuperating revealed both a move as far as they can tell and reaction to negative feelings and sensations just as the improvement of self-administrative aptitudes in managing torment, enthusiastic guideline and re-examination of life circumstances.

PVT offers knowledge into how figuring out how to perceive and move the hidden neural foundation of any given psychophysiological state may legitimately influence physiology, feeling and conduct along these lines helping the individual develop versatile procedures for guideline and flexibility to profit physical, mental and social wellbeing. As mind-body treatments influence the vagal pathways they are proposed to shape methods for "working out" these neural stages to encourage self-guideline and strength of physiological capacity, feeling guideline and prosocial practices.

Ideal neural guideline of the autonomic sensory system and the related endocrine and invulnerable frameworks is encouraged through the dynamic commitment of the VVC by using explicit developments or positions, breathing works on, reciting or contemplation which influences both top-down and base up forms.

Versatility is proposed to be cultivated by both downregulating cautious states and supporting greater adaptability and flexibility in relation to different wonders of the BME to advance physiological rebuilding just as positive mental and social states. The individual can figure out how to improve the actuation of the VVC with its homeostatic effect on the living being, just as increment the office to move all through other neural stages, for example, the SNS or DVC when genuine or saw pressure is experienced.

In total, personality body practices can show the person to make the VVC increasingly open, extend the limit of resilience to other neural stages, change the relationship and reaction to SNS and DVC neural stages that happen as common vacillations of the BME, and how to turn out to be progressively talented at moving all through these neural stages. Breathing moves inside yoga regularly encourage comparable moves in the autonomic state with focalized mental and wellbeing outcomes. These practices may likewise add to our capability to encounter association past social communications or systems and to a progressively all-inclusive and unbounded feeling of unity and association.

SUMMARY

Polyvagal Theory will control you bit by bit through four modules of top to bottom preparing to help you adequately incorporate the transformative intensity of this method and the Social Engagement System in your training. This is what's canvassed in every module:

The Polyvagal Theory

- Principles and highlights of the Polyvagal Theory, and how to apply it in a clinical setting
- How the Polyvagal Theory can demystify a few highlights identified with pressure-related sicknesses and mental issue, for example, PTSD, chemical imbalance, melancholy, and uneasiness
- How the Social Engagement System is undermined by pressure and injury and how to reset it
- Evolutionary changes and versatile capacities in the autonomic sensory system
- Humans' reaction chain of importance to challenges
- Three neural stages that give the neurophysiological bases to social commitment, battle/flight, and shutdown practices

Social Engagement System and Psychiatric and Conductal Disorders

- The "face-heart" association that structures a useful social commitment framework
- How our outward appearances, vocalizations, and signals are controlled by neural components that are engaged with managing our autonomic sensory system

Perception: Detecting and Evaluating Risk

- How our social and physical condition triggers changes in physiological state
- Understanding how versatile physiological responses may bring

about maladaptive practices
- Immobilization unafraid
- Play as a neural exercise and tuning in as a neural exercise
- Fight/flight and immobilization guard methodologies
- The adaptive function of immobilization and the related clinical troubles
- How the burdens and difficulties of life mutilate social mindfulness and dislodge unconstrained social commitment practices with protective responses

Applying the Polyvagal Theory in Clinical Settings
- Understanding sound-related hypersensitivities
- State guideline as a central element of mental issue
- Deconstructing highlights of chemical imbalance and PTSD
- Strategies to clarify disturbance and fix of advantageous guideline
- Identifying expressive gestures that upset or fix cautious response

Convergence of Polyvagal Theory with the *Gunas*

Both PVT and the gunas give a point of view to comprehend fundamental establishments from which physical, mental and social traits rise. PVT gives an understanding into how hidden neural stages are enacted because of saw risk or security within sight of BME marvels. Yoga recommends that physical, mental and conduct properties rise up out of and are affected by the fundamental exchange of the gunas. The two structures examine the conjunction and mixing together of neural stages (PVT) or gunas (Yoga) and endeavor to pass on multifaceted nature in the midst of a characteristic inclination for reductionism inside customary scholarly trains. In PVT, the conjunction of neural stages offers a route to the fluctuated encounters of play (safe preparation) and closeness (safe immobilization). In yoga, the conjunction of the gunas makes the changed marvels of BME and impacts the relationship and response to such boosts. The two speculations encourage that it is from the surfacing of the neural foundation of PVT or the guna of yoga that BME states are made the show and set up.

The gunas of yoga and neural foundation of PVT are additionally reflected in each other in a merged and closely resembling way. This connection between the two models can be seen through the practically identical depictions of properties. At the point when the ANS goes under the impact of one of the gunas a particular neural foundation of the PVT might be initiated supporting shared qualities between the two. In like manner, when a neural stage is actuated, it bolsters the transcendence of a guna and the common attributes between them rise. For instance, when sattva reflects through the sensory system, the physiological, mental, and conduct qualities of the VVC show, or when the VVC is actuated the characteristics of sattva show, as will be depicted in more detail beneath. This exchange investigates the connection between the two models by the way they relate and influence each other for the rise of physical, mental, and social traits. Eventually, this relationship is intended to encourage an understanding that yoga treatment may influence both basic neural stages and gunas, bringing about developed self-guideline and strength for the prosperity of the person.

Poly Faces of Vagus

There are two diverse vagus circuits - a sum of three ANS circuits, not only a couple. The two circuits "originate from two distinct regions of the brain stem, and they advanced successively," one far prior. This spurred me to build up the polyvagal theory, which revealed the life structures and capacity of two vagal frameworks, one conceivably deadly, and the other defensive. "Immobilization, bradycardia, and apnea are segments of an old, reptilian protection framework," Porges says. "In the event that you take a gander at reptiles, you don't see a lot of conduct - on the grounds that immobilization is the essential barrier framework for reptiles… it's an old vagus nerve." This pre-notable nerve has no myelin, a nerve covering of defensive protein and fat. Vertebrates have this unmyelinated vagus, on the dorsal (top) side of the nerve, which immobilizes us, as well "and that immobilization response, versatile for reptiles, is conceivably deadly for warm-blooded creatures.

It was observed that among the "firsts," which started with well-evolved creatures, another vagus with myelin creates on the ventral underside of the nerve. "So warm-blooded creatures have two vagal circuits," he found. "The myelinated circuits give progressively fast and firmly composed reactions. The new mammalian vagus is connected to brain stem zones that direct the muscles of the face and head. Each natural clinician realizes that in the event that they see individuals' appearances and tune in to voices, constrained by muscles of the face and head, they know the physiological condition of their customer."

Neuroception: It's Just Not Cognitive

Our progressively crude neural circuits work by "neuroception" - absolutely automatically. "Neuroception isn't discernment," he says. "Neuroception doesn't require consciousness of things going on. It is discovery without mindfulness. It is a neural circuit that assesses chance in the earth... When gone up against in specific circumstances, a few people experience autonomic reactions, for example, an expansion in pulse and perspiring hands. These reactions are automatic. It doesn't care for they need to do this." The polyvagal theory stresses that our sensory system has more than one safeguard procedure - and whether we use prepared flight/flight or immobilization shutdown, is certifiably not an intentional choice. Outside the domain of our cognizant mindfulness, our sensory system is constantly assessing danger in the earth, making decisions, and organizing practices that are not subjective.

Next, he says, "people and different well evolved creatures, as battle/flight machines, possibly work in the event that they can move and get things done. Yet, on the off chance that we are restricted, in the event that we are set into confinement, or on the off chance that we are lashed down, our sensory system peruses those signs and practically needs to immobilize.

CONCLUSION

In conclusion, the polyvagal theory proposes that the evolution of the mammalian autonomic sensory system gives the neurophysiological substrates to versatile conduct procedures. It further suggests that the physiological state confines the scope of conduct and mental experience. The theory connects the advancement of the autonomic sensory system to full of feeling experience, passionate demeanor, facial signals, vocal correspondence, and unforeseen social conduct. Right now, the theory gives a conceivable clarification to the announced covariation between atypical autonomic guidelines (e.g., decreased vagal and expanded thoughtful impacts to the heart) and mental and conduct issues that include challenges in directing proper social, passionate, and correspondence practices.

The polyvagal theory gives a few experiences into the versatile idea of a physiological state. In the first place, the theory stresses that physiological states bolster various classes of conduct. For instance, a physiological state described by a vagal withdrawal would bolster the preparation practices of battle and flight. Interestingly, a physiological state portrayed by expanded vagal effect on the heart (by means of myelinated vagal pathways starting in the core ambiguous) would support unconstrained social commitment practices. Second, the theory accentuates the arrangement of a coordinated social commitment framework through useful and auxiliary connections between neural control of the striated muscles of the face and the smooth muscles of the viscera. Third, the polyvagal theory proposes an instrument – neuroception - to trigger or to restrain safeguard methodologies.

www.ingramcontent.com/pod-product-compliance
Lightning Source LLC
Chambersburg PA
CBHW052353220526
45465CB00003BA/1093